Dear I

Merry Christmas.

Love you!

Rosa
Dec 17, 2020

Enjoy your visit to Easy Yoke Farm.
Rosemary Ronnlund Belcher
Dec 2020

Suite 300 - 990 Fort St
Victoria, BC, V8V 3K2
Canada

www.friesenpress.com

Copyright © 2020 by Rosemary Ronnlund Belcher
First Edition — 2020

All rights reserved.

No part of this publication may be reproduced in any form, or by any means, electronic or mechanical, including photocopying, recording, or any information browsing, storage, or retrieval system, without permission in writing from FriesenPress.

Some names and descriptions of characters in this book have been changed.

ISBN
978-1-5255-6223-5 (Hardcover)
978-1-5255-6224-2 (Paperback)
978-1-5255-6225-9 (eBook)

1. JUVENILE NONFICTION, ANIMALS, FARM ANIMALS

Distributed to the trade by The Ingram Book Company

Once Upon a Time

Once upon a time is a phrase that usually begins a fairy tale. This time it begins a *wonderful* true story about a family's new adventure of moving far from the city onto a beautiful little farm.

The dream of a farm had begun many years previously, at least in my mind, because I was an animal lover plain and simple. We'd had dogs and cats and birds, all special and beloved, but my animal-loving heart craved more. My name is Rosemary Belcher. I'm the mom who will tell you the happy, hilarious, often exciting and sometimes sad, but true stories about our family's new adventures.

Our family of eight lived in a large city, where soaring mountains, a vast ocean, a mighty river, and sprawling wetlands were a special part of our family's playground. When the sky darkened, twinkling lights on the distant ski lifts brightened the mountainsides and above us, the immense span of God's universe coursed onward in its spectacular beauty.

Inside our home, before bed, and often after enjoying a glance at the night beauty, I was forced to return to urban reality. Softly, I strolled through a home full of sleeping children, returning dangling feet under their covers, murmuring a hushed "'goodnight' to eyes that opened at my approach, and quietly shutting the windows to keep out the ever-increasing roar of fume-laden cars and trucks coursing down the newly-widened street outside our home.

We, the city dwellers, all dreamt of fresh country air, homegrown food, and myriads of friendly, cuddly animals. I have to admit that the last part likely applied mostly to myself and my daughters. However, we couldn't just uproot ourselves and move. We had to wait—wait until Dad retired.

At that time in our lives we had a family that consisted of Mom and Dad and six kids; three boys and three girls.

One snowy winter, our creative boys devised a temporary solution to our traffic problem. They unleashed their usual prankster spirit and built a large snow mound beside the sidewalk on the busy street right at the end of our lawn. I watched with curiosity as they shoveled with more effort than usually went into normal chores. I couldn't hear their comments but knew that this definitely was one of their group efforts. They cleverly shaped the pile like a Volkswagen bug and with much laughter gifted it with discarded VW bumpers and wheels. For many weeks, beckoned by the roar of the approaching snow plow, they skulked behind the living room drapes and giggled and snickered as the driver carefully raised his blade and inched his plow around the precious car so as not to scratch it. Now I have to admit that the rest of the family, including myself and their dad, joined them in their secret and hilarious surveillance. To our pleasure, the traffic also slowed down and carefully avoided the little "bug."

As spring came and the little wonder bug had withstood many small thaws and fresh white coatings, the guilty and we, the co-conspirators, couldn't help but whisper and giggle behind the drapes as we watched and wondered how this practical joke would all end. I don't know why it is that when we were inside and the snow plow was roaring outside that we had to whisper through our group giggles, but it happened, and so it was.

One sunny morning, we knew that our "caper" had ended. The warm night breezes and the morning sun had reduced our precious bug to a fraction of its size. Amazingly, at just the right moment, when the snow plow driver approached with his carefully raised plow blade, the bumpers fell to the ground and a large portion of our little "bug" slid onto the sidewalk. The wide-eyed driver stopped in his tracks, climbed down out of his seat, approached the bumpers and the snow pile, shook his head incredulously, and kicked the bumpers off the road and onto the sidewalk snow pile. He scowled, jumped into his plow, and with furious, enthusiastic gusto, plowed the imaginary bug down the road and off to the side. The noisy traffic resumed its previous freedoms, and we the co-conspirators and the guilty three doubled over in laughter at a very successful joke. Did we feel guilty? Nope! I immediately sent the truly guilty parties out to clear the sidewalk. They weren't as united in this task as they had been when they built the bug, and I distinctly remember some grumbling words, which I won't repeat.

Now I must tell you more about the Belcher family journey towards moving to the farm, and in the process, I will help you to get to know our kids.

The three clever pranksters were our sons, Paul, David, and Rob. They were my little boy "gang" that I loved raising, but they were almost full grown at this point and had had lots of time to practice their art of group conspiracy.

Our three lovely daughters, one of whom was quickly approaching her wedding day, were just as creative, if not more so. They, along with my boys, had made me a happy and busy mom.

My husband, Thomas, and I had been married for a long time. At the writing of this book we have passed fifty years. He worked as a technical specialist for a computer company, but he was thinking of retiring and an idea began to tingle in our brains. Like me, he also wanted to get out of the city and had a few ideas about where he would like us to resettle.

I wanted a farm, with lots of animals. I wanted to learn how to milk, make cheese, soap, and candles, and have a big garden (that I wouldn't have to weed), and must I repeat, have lots of animals. My dad had grown up on a farm in northern Sweden and I loved to hear his stories.

THE REAL TAILS OF EASY YOKE FARM

Our younger girls, Crystal and Melody, shared my dreams.

Thomas's business trips were mainly to distant places and we missed him dearly whenever he was gone. When he went on small business trips in the province, the two younger girls and I often tagged along. We had developed a routine:

The phone rang with Thomas calling. "I have to head up to…Honey, would you and the girls like to come along?"

"Absolutely," I responded.

"Okay, I'll be home in less than an hour, could you all pack and be ready?"

"No problem!" I answered, excited that we could all get away for a bit. "Girls! Dad's going to be home in less than an hour. Do you want to go on a business trip with him?"

"Yeeeaaah!" I heard the girls cheering and knew that they were jumping up and down in excitement wherever they were in the house.

"Time to pack up, then" I reminded them, even though I already heard feet scrambling to get ready. "Dad will be home soon, and he wants to get on the road right away!"

The machines that Thomas was sent to fix had usually gone through a number of servicemen already. Dad was one of the "big guns" and last resorts that the company sent out to calm frustrated customers and get them back to running their businesses again.

"Okay Mom, we're packing!" I always heard in a united, jubilant response from both girls. I could hear the commotion as they joyfully raced around their room and quickly packed from their basic list of quick-trip clothing. I also knew that their two beloved, scruffy Teddies, Coocoo and Crummy would already be stuffed into a suitcase.

I'll give you an example of one such trip:

"Should we bring our bathing suits?" called Crystal from her room.

"Yes," I answered, "and some large towels; one for each of us…Oh get the sun screen and the mosquito repellent too." I headed to our bedroom and packed from our list, remembering to add Thomas's and my bathing suits to the suitcase.

"Mom, can we pack the whale?" Melody called from downstairs.

The whale was a huge blow-up water toy that we all could sit on in the water, at least for a few moments before someone tipped it and we all fell off.

"Yes, and the foot pump," I answered, hearing footsteps heading out to the garage to search for the huge, carefully folded and boxed beach toy.

After the main quick pack, we all ended up in the kitchen. Melody arrived lugging the big boxed blue whale. The foot pump with the hose was stuck under her arm, and the rest banged on her knee with each step. She was also struggling to hold onto the picnic cooler and juice jug that she had discovered in with the camping stuff.

"I've got some things for the cooler," Crystal called on her last few steps up from the pantry. She unloaded her armful onto the kitchen counter, stooping to pick up a few granola bars that had slipped onto the floor. She had raided the pantry for granola bars, juice boxes, a package of cookies, and our travel pack of plastic cutlery, plates, glasses and tiny cutting board.

Things were progressing nicely; my experienced daughters seemed to be remembering everything.

I scanned our resources that had been gathered up to this point. When I saw the apple juice boxes I had to smile as a memory flash of another road trip crossed my busy mind.

The kids were a bit younger and our two Brittany spaniels, Cookie and Candy, had accompanied us in our van. Mid-afternoon, I passed out juice boxes and cracker packs, and all was going well. But then we heard poor Candy whining desperately to be let out. Cookie, the other dog, seemed fine.

We stopped the van along the side of the road in a grassy area, and all piled out. But the poor dog just stood there in the wide open door and shook. We just stared at her in wonder until one of the boys gently picked her up and set her down on the side of the road.

I hate to say it, but it's a memory ingrained into all of our minds. She really had to go! That dog made a yellow stream that continued and continued. The entire family stood and stared at the gully in the dry ground where flash flooding was taking place for half a dozen feet along the highway.

I looked at Tom with eyebrows raised then turned to the kids. "Has she been drinking?" I asked.

We always carried a water dish with us but as far as I knew the dogs had only had a few licks about an hour ago.

Melody's small voice finally replied; "Mommy. I couldn't drink all my juice so I put in into her dish and she liked it."

Then, sounding a little more confident than her sister, Crystal admitted, "I gave her the rest of mine too, I didn't want to waste it."

After a lengthy confessional we discovered that all six kids had donated what likely amounted to four cups of apple juice to the poor, unsuspecting but willing spaniel.

"Well what about Cookie?" I asked looking at the unaffected, frolicking pup tugging playfully on her leash.

"Cookie doesn't like apple juice," came Crystal's innocent reply.

Finally, the relieved dog began to wag her little tail once more and jumped happily into the van. Our road trip continued along with my firm warning, "Don't any of you give the dogs your leftover juice!"

Still standing in the kitchen and waiting for Thomas to arrive home, I shook my head and smiled at the fond memories. This time the dogs would be staying home with the boys, who would be home from school and work later in the day.

I added bread and a few other things to the cooler, just as Thomas entered the front door.

"Daddy, Daddy, Dad's here!" came the announcement.

His car was loaded in moments and our trip towards possible new homes and farms began.

As always on our "business trips" we took the time to go down back-country roads, explore villages, and slow down when we passed "For Sale" signs nailed to rural fence posts.

"I wonder what it would be like to live there?" I asked.

"It would be an awful long way to get groceries," Thomas responded.

"We could just shop once a month," Crystal chimed in.

"We could have our own cow and milk and cheese and stuff and a horse," Melody added with smiling eyes and a faraway, dreamy expression.

"We'll have a big garden," Crystal our plant-loving gardener exclaimed with the same dreamy expression that accompanied her sister's horse dream. "And, I want some sheep," she added with a grin.

She'd been learning how to crochet, make bobbin lace, and quilt. The thought of sheep was wonderful and the vision of endless batting, homemade wool, and getting a spinning wheel was joyfully overwhelming.

Thomas, who was constantly in teaching mode, stopped the car near a clump of some kind of wild grain. He got out, leaned over, pulled a handful of stalks, and went over to the window where the girls were peering out with interest. He showed them the ripe stalks and instructed them, "These are wild oats, girls." He carefully turned the oats in his hands and handed the little bundle to the outstretched hand reaching from the now-open window.

Thomas turned to me; the wife whom he had married so young, and with a wink said, "I never got a chance to sow my wild oats, honey."

With big blue eyes, Crystal, the innocent little gardener offered, "I'll sow them for you, Daddy!"

We adults continue to smile at that memory.

We passed many ramshackle houses that I thought were ready for a bulldozer. Melody looked carefully over them and then sincerely exclaimed from the depths of her adventurous pioneer heart, "I could live there!"

Of course, we all disagreed, but the stars still twinkled in her eyes as she turned her head for one more glance behind us.

Back then, Melody was a sweetly contented little girl, who was as relaxed as a sack of cotton. At present, she is a happy mom. She's living on a farm, off-grid with her big country family in eastern Canada, and loving it.

Our searching and questions continued every time we saw the next "For Sale" sign with its endless new possibilities.

In town, while Thomas repaired failing business systems, the girls and I scouted little shops and read all the real estate ads we could find. Trip after joyous trip, our dreams began to gel into what our future lives might be like.

Now, it has been mentioned that Crystal wanted sheep and Melody wanted a horse, but there was also one very specific animal on my list. I had to make an adjustment to my desires, because I really wanted a camel. Yes, I love camels. I figured that the closest animal that I could find would be a llama. A great big llama!

I liked BIG, and I wanted a challenge. But, the question was, how would I, a mom who didn't work at a job where I could earn money, pay for an exotic animal like a llama? At this time, llamas were in high demand, and very expensive. You could buy a car for less than you would pay for a llama back then. How could I make some money?

But one day, a few weeks before, when I had been cleaning up the house, I looked around. My kids had just come in from school. I could tell—it was very obvious. The space by the front door was heaped with coats, some on the floor, some dragging from the top of the railing, and there were piles of boots, shoes, purses, backpacks, school books, a trumpet case, a few half-crumpled empty lunch bags, school flyers, and some toques and scarves.

I had begged, complained, and pleaded, but that front-door stair landing was always impassable. I sighed a big sigh…and then smiled. I had just figured out how to earn an income!

I would charge a fee for all items that were neither hung up neatly, placed on a boot rack, put in the garbage, or put away in bedrooms.

I found a box and made a slit. I covered it with pretty paper, and wrote in large felt-tip pen letters, "MOM'S LLAMA FUND." After clearing off the heap that was on top of the little table near the door onto the floor, I placed the box on the table.

We had a little Belcher family meeting at the dinner table that night. I was all smiles. I could see my wonderful new llama grazing out in my dreamed-of farm pasture, and it was wonderful. I announced, "There are going to be some changes around here."

There were mass groans.

"See this little box?" It was actually a shoebox with ample room for lots of donations to my worthy cause. I held it out and moved my arm around the table to make sure that everyone had a good look. "You all know that we would love to move out to the country and get a nice farm someday."

A few smiles snuck onto faces, but they all knew that something was coming that they might not like.

"You also know that I really want a llama."

A few raised faces were attentive to me in a bored kind of way.

"This box is my llama fund. This is where the money will be put that will buy me a llama when we move to the farm!"

My intended victims were still watching but continued to clean their plates.

"You will be buying me my llama!"

There were some hard swallows and suddenly all the faces, with mouths full or empty, stared at me with wide eyes.

Now I truly had their attention. "This box is going to sit on the little table next to the front door." My voice became stern. "You know, the one that you can never see because of the piles of clothes and junk on it!"

Faces were beginning to flush and eyes began to glance sideways at each other with a *Here it comes* look.

"Beginning this evening, every piece of clothing and all the school books, binders, shoes, gym bags, instruments, school notices, old lunch bags, etc. will have their owners found and each item will be worth one quarter, which will go into my box."

The kids were in shock! They looked at the box and then, even though they couldn't see through the wall, their eyes turned towards the front door with horror. I could pretty much see the dollar signs swimming and then drowning in their fearful brains as they realized just how much they each would have to pay me.

I set the box down, and calmly continued eating. Point made!

"Mom, can I please be excused?" a guilty party asked.

I saw that dinner was basically over and nodded. "Yes."

"Me too, Mom," came a second query, and then the rest of the requests to leave the table arrived. The requests piled upon each other as much as the things in the heap at the front door.

The race was on! Kids scrambled down those stairs and grabbed their stuff so fast that they knocked each other over, pushing and shoving. There were cries of:

"No that's mine!"

"No, it's not, that's yours over there."

"Here, take your stuff off my coat."

These cries resonated up into the kitchen where I was clearing the table. As I turned, I was sure that I could see a cloud of dust rising up from the stairwell, like when a herd of buffalo stampedes in a Western movie. But that would be admitting to poor housekeeping on my part, so I dismissed the thought.

In moments, it was over and quiet. I peered down the stairwell and watched my last victim, a daughter. She not only grabbed her scarf, she turned to straighten the table and replaced the crooked doily before she disappeared like a frightened rabbit. Daughters are so nice to have around.

I felt pretty cocky. I looked over at my hubby with a *How did you like that?* kind of look. He shrugged a *We'll see* sort of shrug and headed into the living room. He was quite accustomed to my little "kid control" projects. Some worked and some didn't. I'm sure that most of them worked.

Over the next few days, the front doorway remained much cleaner and empty of forbidden items. Then, the clutter returned. So, I began passing my box around as soon as the kids came through the door. I was catching them in the act as they flung down their belongings. I wasn't popular at all. My little box now had a distinct jingle to it and was feeling heavier each day. Eventually, the kids finally got the idea that Mom wasn't giving up and the entranceway began to stay clean. I was a bit smug and assumed that the battle had been eternally won.

One morning, after the horde had left for school and work, I checked my front landing with a smile. A bolt of great concern shot over me. Something was wrong! Yes, the area was clear of clutter. But! My box was GONE! In its place sat a letter.

I raced down the stairs, grabbed the letter, and in surprise had to sit back on a stair to read it. I couldn't believe my eyes. Although I can't remember the words exactly the general and pretty correct gist was this:

THE REAL TAILS OF EASY YOKE FARM

> *Mom*
>
> *"We have taken your box.*
> *You, the rich, have been stealing from us, the poor, and so we have taken it to give back to the poor—us!*
>
> *Signed:*
> *The Sheriff of Nottingham [now identified as my dear son, Rob]*
> *Robin Hood- [next son, Paul]*
> *Friar Tuck [youngest son, David]*
> *Little John- [Melody]*
> *Maid Marion, [Crystal]*

Of course they didn't let me know who was who at that time, But a mother has her suspicions.

The front door landing remained clear. My llama-fund box remained GONE. I knew my kids were not truly thieves at heart. So, after a day or two I thought that maybe the joke had run its course.

I decided to ask them about it. "Where is my llama-fund box?"

There were slight snickers and small eye movements glancing at each other from the side.

" Guys," I repeated with my voice rising." Where is my box?!" I was now a bit concerned that maybe they had redistributed my wealth among themselves. But I just couldn't believe that they would go that far. Surely they would know that there would be some major repercussions if they had.

"Gone," came an almost straight-faced reply from the one I suspected was the ringleader: the Sheriff of Nottingham.

The others quietly snickered and lowered their faces—as if I didn't know!

"I collected that money fair and square," I said firmly. "When you have that landing cluttered with things that don't belong there, it's not only an eyesore, but it is a tripping hazard that could end someone up in the hospital."

"But Mom, it's not fair!" the sheriff complained bitterly. "It's getting so expensive! It's taking all of our allowances just for your box!"

There was a group whine, a groan, and some nodding of doleful heads.

"Well," I replied with even greater firmness, "then, pick up your stuff or simply take it directly into your rooms and sort it out there! Now, I want my box back, with all of the money in it!" I gave them all a Mom glare that showed that I meant business.

There was a low, group-groan of defeat, and I think that it was Robin Hood, or maybe it was Friar Tuck who got up, fetched the still-jingly box, and with downcast eyes handed it back to me.

The front door area remained clean, but my llama box didn't get any more donations either. It was one of those win/lose situations.

After many years had passed, along with many road trips, a good retirement offer finally came in earnest. Our family sincerely prayed about what we should do. Life's decisions are too serious to be made without taking the time for a good consultation with our Creator and loving Heavenly Father.

He showed us clearly that this was the time to go forward. Within a period of mere weeks, Thomas and I were headed north to scout out the area where we had decided that we should settle down for our new lives.

Our home in the south was listed with a real-estate agent and David, now a young adult, along with Crystal and Melody, who were young teens, were left to housesit and relay messages.

To make a long story short, at a time when houses weren't selling, the Lord sold our house for the price that we had asked. Up North, we found a beautiful, perfect, little farm that more than met all of our dreams and needs. We headed home and packed.

Moving a big household is not an easy task.

Everybody has their personal treasures that no one else cares about. Thomas's company had three different moving companies come in to give a cost estimate and they all came in pretty close to each other. Amazingly, between the bunch of us, we had 2000 pounds of books. I also had a very full pantry where the girls and I had canned so many fruits and veggies and pickles. I had decided that they needed to know this important life skill, so we had spent a lot of time learning how to can safely. I wasn't about to leave my precious preserves or jars, so they had to be packed as well.

Canning pears had been so much fun that summer. As we worked in our sticky, juicy kitchen we talked in pear language. "Apearently this one was rotten!"

"Our pearents definitely wouldn't like to eat rotten fruit," came the reply with the giggle.

"I've been working so hard that I am feeling Impeared," came another comment along with a phony faint.

"Here give me the other pearing knife, I want to expeariment with it.

"Mom I'm hungry, could you prepear lunch soon?"

It went on and on. Their inspearation was endless and we laughed through many lovely filled jars.

On moving day, the chosen van line arrived and we basically just stood back and tried to stay out or their way. Box after box filled the front yard and was loaded into the huge waiting van with the gaping interiors. The sky became dark before they were finished loading. The last decision was where they would put my husband's two handmade cedar canoes.

One eventually fit into the trailer, but the beautiful freighter that fit all of us, our dogs, and gear, fit nowhere. Finally, the driver had a great idea and tied it to the roof of the cab with its end protruding like the beak of an enormous eagle.

They took pictures because they had never tied a canoe to their van before. That picture with the canoe beak still sits on the wall of the moving company after more than twenty-five years.

The next morning, in great excitement, we all drove away together. Thomas drove our family van; with Paul; Crystal; Melody; our dog, Candy, (Cookie was now frisking around the grassy heavenly dog park); a large cage full of Melody's Australian zebra finches; and our old cat. I drove David's little jeep, pulling a trailer, and he rode shotgun.

The trip seemed to take forever. Numerous people had asked why we would want to move to "that God-forsaken place." They warned of blizzards, mosquitoes, and ugly surroundings. We ignored them, knowing that God was taking our family to a special place that He had chosen just for us. We didn't have to worry.

Two days later, Thomas stopped the lead van at the edge of the highway and said, "Kids, this is it!"

A beautiful little farm lay nestled just in view.

"Who would like to get out and pull down the 'Sold' sign off of the fence?"

There were a number of takers and that sign was ripped down in moments. We drove down the beautiful, long, tree-lined driveway and parked well to the side. Within a few moments a very large, long moving van was struggling to turn off the side road and into our yard. Thomas and the boys rushed out to direct the first move of the day, and the girls and I went exploring. Of course, I had been there before, but seeing their eyes sparkle and the huge smiles on their faces told me that the Lord had found us the home that we had all dreamed of.

Trust in the LORD with all thine heart; and lean not unto thine own understanding.
In all thy ways acknowledge him,
and he shall direct thy paths. Proverbs 3:5,6

Like the beak of an enormous eagle.

Farm Home at Last

The Belcher family had finally arrived at our new home, a lovely old farmhouse. We were all exhausted from the long trip but within moments Thomas and I, Paul and David, Crystal and Melody were breathing in fresh country air. We all gazed at the beauty and listened to the quietness around us with huge smiles on our faces and thanksgiving in our hearts.

Suddenly, the loud roar of an engine and sighing brakes told us that the moving van had arrived. The guys jogged back out to the road to try to escort the long moving truck down the narrow-curved, tree-lined driveway.

Crystal and Melody had other ideas and rushed into the house opening every door and peeking into every room. I followed quickly behind them, smiling at their joy. They walked through the sunroom, twirling before the long windows to enjoy the sun's warmth that was pouring in.

"This is where my bird cages will go!" Melody decided quickly, grinning widely. Then she remembered that her feathered companions still waited in their cages in the van beside the cat cage that held the frustrated family cat.

"We could put lots of plants here, it could be like a jungle," Crystal laughed. "And we could start lots of plants out here in the spring for our garden." She followed her sister down to the end of the room.

Melody was sliding a steamy glass door open and breathing in the warm, moist heat of the beautiful, cedar-clad room.

"Look at this!" Look at our hot tub!" she cried. "I can't wait to get into it."

The previous owner had filled and left a fresh tub of inviting water that sparkled in the sunlight filtering in through the large windows. Crystal gingerly pushed a button on a little panel and the water churned to life.

"Ooooooh!" came the excited gasp. Both girls jumped back giggling and then buried their arms to the elbows in the steamy bubbles.

"Come on!" Melody called, flicking the water off her arms. She was already heading into the living room.

Before us was a large fireplace and wide chimney. Its mantle was a twelve-foot-long chunk of solid wood more than a foot square. It hung over the wide, dark opening and then curved slightly around the sides.

I imagined the cute ornaments and pictures that I could set on it, as well as the wonderful place that it would be for hanging Christmas stockings.

The girls noticed the bay window and the entire wall of heavily-lined, rust-colored, velvet curtains topped with large swags. "Wow," came their gasp of approval. "These are beautiful!"

"These should keep the cold out," I commented, nodding, and I hoped that they really would. We had been told that things got very cold up here in the north. The opening at the other end of the living room led to a roomy entranceway at the front door. The door itself was a solid white, but a lovely, glass storm-door that was etched with what looked like delicate hoar frost kept the drafts out.

Across from the living room was the master bedroom, with solid old maple floors, and large windows at the side and head. Farther along the hallway was a large bathroom, with old fixtures and a pedestal sink. There was a small laundry room that I knew would quickly become an office, a dining room that eased up against the patio windows, and finally a lovely oak kitchen.

The lower floor was the first stop, but I could already hear footsteps running up the narrow stairs. The girls had found their bedroom. I knew that it was nice and roomy with hidden storage eaves. One side was graced by a unique, swooped ceiling that followed the curvature of the roof. Pretty, old-fashioned wallpaper and sweet curtains completed the perfect wish list for my daughters, who loved old-fashioned things. The happy chatter echoing down the stairs told me that they both loved it.

Beside the stairs was a small open room that begged to be a sitting area, and ended with what the locals called our sleepy-eye window. The window had a little rounded roof over it that looked like an eyebrow.

The large bedroom at the front of the house boasted a brick chimney at its center. A wood stove had been used to keep its sleepers warm and cozy. This would be the boys' room. It overlooked the front yard and driveway.

After having found their bedroom, the girls headed quickly out to the barnyard.

I was sure that they would be pleased to discover what was waiting for them in the barn. The previous owner had asked us if we would continue to care for a few barn cats that had never been any trouble but kept the mice at bay. I agreed and expected to find a couple of kitties in the barn.

Our new barn was a picture-perfect red barn with white trim. It had two new end stalls, and stairs to an upper storage room where square hay bales and feed could be stored.

"Awwwwww," came the sound from the barn. *The girls found the kitties*, I thought. They had found the kitties! There were at least two of all ages, colors and sizes crouched and warily watching us from each step of the barn that led to the upper loft.

There had to have been way more than fifteen cats. They were all adorable but completely wild and unable to be petted. I had been told that they had their purpose and place, so we began feeding them and the girls began spending lots of time trying to tame them.

The big ole fluffy cat that we had brought from our previous home would be staying in the house.

As the girls headed for the pasture, I stood momentarily and watched the huge antique windmill slicing gently through the breezes. This was such a perfect place! The old windmill creaked loudly, whined, and then with a loud *kachunk* wheeled around and faced another direction. A long rod in the middle of its strong girders moved rhythmically up and down as the windmill blades turned.

Windmill at dawn.

Crystal and Melody were already in the pastures. I'm sure that they were imagining all the animals that would live there one day.

The gasp and whine of air brakes reminded us that this was moving day and that the moving truck had finally managed to squeeze up to the back door. The moving men climbed down from the cab and stretched.

The girls and I hurried to make sure that the birdcages were moved inside. The old cat and Candy, the dog, were escorted to safe out-of-the-way places in the house. Thomas, David, and Paul began directing the movers. Moving boxes began piling up on the driveway, filling the sunroom, and finding their ways to their proper rooms according to their labels.

Oh boy, I thought. *Oh boy*—that was about the only thing that would come to my tired mind. The work ahead of us, even to set up beds, find bed linens, find something to eat, and settle down for the night was overwhelming.

Over the next days the boxes were emptied, things found their places,

and our family excitedly explored more of our new home. We discovered and began to harvest the huge, well-kept garden that covered the entire west side of the lot. There were potatoes the size of bread loaves, beets like softballs, huge cabbages, peas, beans, and carrots, and rows of lettuce, radishes, and onions both green and round. Tomatoes clinging to well-kept vines overflowed the front part of the garden.

Farther back and closer to the road grew many rows of strawberries, tall raspberry bushes on wooden trellises, and a fragrant lilac bush that hedged the entire roadside of the property. Beyond the lilacs, a three-board white farm fence edged the entire farm with the exception of the long creek bank at the base of the hill. We had come to paradise, and the harvest more than filled a beautifully constructed basement cold room to the brim. We were truly blessed.

We knew that this was the beginning of a new life and adventure for all of us and we thanked the Lord as a family and planned a special day.

One Saturday we took a walk. We hiked the property line around the entire farm; around the edge of the barnyard and pastures, through the trees, along the muddy creek bank, and hugging the fence line back up to the road and into the driveway once again. As we struggled and laughed through the areas without paths, our hearts were full of thanksgiving and we stopped to prayerfully give our farm back to the Lord for His protection and use. Now we could all settle down and enjoy our new adventure.

As we decorated our new home, we hung a lovely farm scene in the sunroom that had the following beautiful verses painted on it:

Be thou diligent to know the state of thy flocks,
and look well to thy herds.
The lambs are for thy clothing, and the goats
are the price of the field.
And thou shalt have goats' milk enough for thy food,
for the food of thy household, and for
the maintenance of thy maidens.
Proverbs 27; 23,26,27

ROSEMARY RONNLUND BELCHER

A beautiful little farm lay nestled just in view.

The Swimming Hole and the Watching Eyes

The weather was still warm and our new lands begged to be explored. Curiosity took us on many walks and explorations. Behind the house and the lovely stretch of well-tended lawn stood a long stand of trees that guarded the entire rear of the property. The farmyard was open to sight and sunshine. The woods appeared dark, they seemed to be hiding something. You could just sense it as you peered towards them. Maybe it was just that we were from the city, but there was always an eerie feeling that something was there. Something that was watching us.

From the farmhouse, we could hear the trembling-aspen leaves fluttering and whispering in the warm breezes. As we approached the coolness of the small forest, the tall blackgreen spruce waved and groaned. When the evening winds rose, the darkness creaked and cracked with the huge limbs lashing out against each other, whipping off branches, and roaring in anger. In these woods, bears, both black and brown, roamed and foraged. They grunted as they lumbered up and down the slopes, scratched the tree bark, ate the berries, and bedded down in their secret dugouts in the hill—our hill! There were cougars that travelled down the creek a few times a year. The previous owners had given us a firm warning to watch out for the large cats, who were not afraid to come up into the yard and farmyard. The farm woods were a place of beauty, intrigue, and sometimes fear.

Beyond the treeline, a narrow path twisted downward through a concealed natural garden of, trilliums, tiny dogwoods, and miniscule wildflowers. The little-travelled trail often disappeared into clumped grass, fallen leaves, and branches and then reappeared past bumpy, mossy tree roots.

It was a slippery and often ankle-twisting little journey. It twined towards the sound of water rushing over slippery rocks and gurgling and splashing against the uneven shores.

At the bottom of the trail was a clear and busy creek. It was fed through a large fresh water culvert that escorted its flow from a nearby lake and sparkled invitingly in the

The woods appeared dark. They seemed to be hiding something.

sunshine. The water poured out of the culvert like a waterfall, burying itself deeply in a whirlpool and then springing to life once again a few feet downwards.

Although the woods felt eerie and unnerving, the stream below was nature's magnet. The kids found the whirlpool to be their own personal waterpark. They slid down the opposite bank into the whirlpool. Like a pack of otters, they disappeared and then bobbed up like apples just down the stream.

As they played and swam, they found that more than water was pouring through that culvert—many good-sized fish had discovered the warm pools that the kids loved. The lazy fish were often caught in the kids' hands and brought wriggling up to the dinner table.

On many days, above their laughter, the kids heard a loud crack. Like a big gun had just gone off.

"What was that?" Melody asked looking back into the dark woods.

"I don't know," replied Crystal. "It sounded like a big gun! Maybe someone's hunting down stream?"

"Well, I hope that they stay down there," Melody replied.

The woods were quiet once again, and the water invited more playing and swimming.

Eventually, it was time to head back up to the farm. The walk was unnerving, because although the creek was bathed in sunlight, the path back up to the farm wound through the sunless shade of the dark trees. Was someone or something watching? It was a path that you wanted to hurry along, and you only breathed comfortably once again when you reached the grassy lawn.

The kids spent hours swimming down at the creek during the warm summers- ending. When it became too warm in the fall sun, they began repairing the shady, twisty path by lining its sides with stream-rounded stones. They often returned up the path with lovely wildflower bouquets for my table.

More than one swimmer with a towel-covered bottom confessed that the constant sliding down the slippery dirt bank into the pool had worn through their bathing suits and I heard, "Mom, I need a new bathing suit!"

During the joyous times of work and play, that loud sharp *crack*, would often pierce the air, sending shivers down each of our spines. I could easily hear it up on top. It was very loud in the woods. I was really concerned that maybe hunters were in our woods shooting at the ever-present deer and other wildlife. I didn't want my kids ending up with gunshot wounds. I comforted myself that with all of the noise that they usually made, they probably wouldn't get mistaken for anything but noisy kids at play.

Still, I warned them all soundly. "Please be really careful when you go down to the creek! We don't really know what's down there yet. I don't want you all shot or even eaten! Look out for each other!"

As the autumn approached, we noticed another farm phenomenon; the bank on the opposite side of the creek became bare of trees. Only the grasses and some short bushes remained and our bank was also getting bare.

Someone was cutting off our lovely tall trees about three feet from their bases and carting them away. *Surely, they could find a better place to collect firewood,* I mused. There was something going on that none of us liked.

There was someone down there who was very busy, and was watching us to make sure that we never saw them—someone who was ruining our land.

"Let's go for a walk tonight," I suggested to Thomas. "We could head down the creek where we've never been before."

"I guess so," he replied, and we decided to tell the kids at dinner time.

"Do you kids want to go for a walk tonight?" Thomas asked. "We're going to head down the creek and see what's there."

"Okay."

"Sure."

So we all agreed.

The farm and the air seemed very peaceful and still that evening as we began our trek by walking comfortably down the nicely groomed trail.

"You guys have done a really nice job on this trail," Thomas commented.

I agreed. "It's so nice to be able to walk without tripping over something!"

Halfway down, we veered to the east and began our struggle through the low brush and foliage. Fighting our way along the weedy, muddy creek edge we were excited to see just what lay beyond our property. In my opinion as a mom, we were making enough noise to stay safe. Before long we came upon a sight that raised the curiosity and enjoyment in all of us. Poking out of the water like a huge, upturned bowl peeked a large beaver lodge.

"Beavers!" came the hushed and excited whisper.

"Shh, shhh, shh! They'll hear us!" came the hushed group whispers from all of us.

It seemed that we all had the same idea.

"Let's hide, over here, and wait quietly and see what's going on."

We ducked and crunched down in little family clumps among the bushes and tried not to noisily swat at the ever-present mosquitoes. After we had all settled in our places, the only sounds remaining were the evening prayers of the robins and the gurgling of the stream.

Suddenly, the quiet was shattered! Just up the bank behind us, we heard a rustling. We froze, almost fearing to breathe. We thought of the dreaded bears or the cougars and hoped that the noise wasn't coming from one of them. The crackling of leaves and breaking of tiny branches became louder and louder. Then a dark form quickly slithered down the hill, passing us only six feet from our hiding place. It slipped into the water and disappeared. Some of us clung to each other a little closer, staring with wide, excited eyes. Then we settled back into our positions and warily continued our surveillance.

More rustling—this time a little louder and rougher. Something huge and bulky was heading down the hill behind us. We scrunched up our shoulders, squinting our eyes, and hoping for the best.

IT was approaching closer and closer!

Along the same path travelled by the first dark form burst a tree. Its end was about four inches wide, followed by all its branches dragging behind it.

"A tree is coming down the hill," whispered Paul. "A whole tree!"

Truly, a tree was-barreling-down-the-hill at an amazing pace.

We all turned our heads and saw two dark creatures straining and grunting and finally dragging the tree down to the water. They floated and swam with it until it lay before the lodge with its stump stuck on a small muddy island.

The two busy workers disappeared under the stream and the big guy, the first slitherer, reappeared. He swam around the newly fallen tree, and perched up on the little mud island. He stood up on his hind legs and we saw that he was easily more than three feet tall. His coat was dark, rough, and wet. The tubby fellow surveyed the creek bank and then slowly turned to stare right at our hiding place with piercing, beady eyes.

"He knows we're here!" whispered Melody.

"Shhh!" came more than one warning.

His stare was long and chilling. He knew that we were there alright!

Suddenly, he grunted loudly and slapped that huge flat tail across the water with a vengeance. SMACK! This swarthy beaver was the "gunshot" we'd been hearing.

We had beavers! Boy, did we have beavers!

We were delighted and awestruck. We looked at each other with the delight of finding a treasure. This city family had their own clan of beavers.

The beavers had work to do, and they weren't particularly bothered by our presence. As we watched, the soaked and furry workers scuttled up and down the bank. Often, they were within feet of us, gnawing off choice aspen branches and dragging them down to "Papa Beaver," the crew boss and tail smacker.

It felt like hours passed. Then, darkness crept in on us and although the beaver family worked on, we knew that we had better head for home before one of us twisted an ankle on the trip back.

We hiked up the hill and sat in the warm farm kitchen drinking cocoa. There was much to talk about—we were all so excited, but all so tired. It was time for bed.

There were no hunters, just some fat, furry, and determined beavers.

That night I lay awake. The beavers were kind of cute, although large and burly. Our city friends would certainly be interested to hear about them. As I thought about the determined little loggers, I began to worry about our precious trees that shaded our treed bank.

Surely these beavers would run out of trees just past the property and continue their onslaught of logging right below our noses.

The next morning, I headed to the hardware store. I purchased rolls of wire that looked like a mesh of big wire squares. It's usually called page wire. I also purchased a number of pairs of work gloves.

At dinner, I announced the necessary defence of our new farm. On Saturday morning, the kids headed down to the creek loaded with the new supplies. For a number of days, they wrapped wire around every whispering aspen in our little forest. Yes, it was hard work, but I figured that four-foot of page wire just might send the furry woodsmen onto other logging grounds. The kids groaned but worked like beavers and the trees seemed secure.

The beaver logging on our hill stopped and I felt quite happy until I looked out at our lovely yard one Saturday morning.

There, on our nice lawn amongst our special and ornamental yard trees, stood Papa Beaver. He waddled around with impunity sniffing the fall air. Then, he stood up to his full height, put his little paws on one of my lovely trees, and pressed his furry nose up to the trunk. Sniffing deeply, he rambled around the tree, and sniffed in another spot. He then waddled over to another; a lovely mountain ash, in full berry. He stood up once again, and sniffed deeply.

I had had enough! The nerve of him, coming up into my yard and sniffing my yard trees. He wasn't going to log my yard, and I wasn't going to have page wire all over my trees either.

I raced out onto the grass and with hands on hips told Papa Beaver, "You leave my yard right now, go on, get! And never come up here again!"

He looked at me calmly, intently, and fearlessly. Then he turned and slowly dragged his sizable tail across my lawn and over to the fence. He slipped with a splash down into the ditch and disappeared.

What a nerve, I thought.

The loud cracks in the forest continued, and we knew that it was just Papa Beaver directing his family in their lodge building. It wasn't a secret that the beavers were there; they had devastated most of the hills around us. But our little forest remained lush, cool, and green. They might watch our family just like we watched theirs, they might smack their tails in frustration, but logging had better happen somewhere else. As for the bear and cougars, well, it was time that we remembered that we had a loving Heavenly Father who watched over us. He was probably amused at our fear of those furry little beasts. We had given our farm to Him and it was time for us to rest in His care and not worry about things that we had no control over.

> *I will both lay me down in peace,*
> *and sleep: for thou, LORD,*
> *only makest me dwell in safety. Psalm 4:8*

Waxwings in a Pickle

We began to notice changes in our surroundings. The whispering aspens donned an intense apricot gold, the low bushes wore burgundy, the mountain ash tree abounded with red berries, and crimson swaths of color adorned the farm.

"Wow, honey," Thomas called one morning on his way out the door. "Come and see the beautiful trees!"

I went out the door into the driveway. The autumn colors were not only bright, but in places the colors seemed almost fluorescent.

"That's amazing!" I responded. "God has brought us to such a beautiful place." I gave Thomas a kiss and goodbye hug and off he drove.

Over the next week, the breezes began to stir in the treetops. The lovely trees wept for the disappearing summer warmth and flooded the ground with piles of autumn leaves.

The Canada geese were also sensing the changing season and began to gather in the neighbouring fields. They mounted up into the air, looping around in short practice flights, and then landing once again.

One evening when the moon was bright and the air chilly, loud honking broke the silence. Running to the windows we looked skyward. The flock had risen in flight. The geese from neighbouring fields had joined their ranks and now massive flocks winged their way southward. A rhythmic whooshing and flapping of heavy wings filled the air, their feathers whistling, and raucous, joyous honking engulfed the sky.

"Kids, come quickly and see the geese," Thomas called, and we gathered shivering in the driveway with eyes scanning the wide country sky.

We didn't need to be quick. The massive goose parade carried on and on. Strong snow geese with the moonlight glimmering on their snow-white wings had joined the flock and flew in droves along with their feathered friends. Flight upon flight passed over. It seemed as though every goose in the world had gathered to travel together on this chilly evening. For almost two hours the amazing flypast continued. We watched spellbound until the last smaller group caught up and honked its way out of sight. What we didn't know was that these massive birds, whose much-awaited entrance heralded the spring, were drawing the last breath of warmth away from the North. That very night, the ground froze, Snow pellets danced in the air and winter had come.

Inside we were warm and cozy. Even Melody's Australian zebra finches in their roomy cages nested comfortably in the warm sunroom.

THE REAL TAILS OF EASY YOKE FARM

The morning after the geese had flown, we heard a new kind of bird song. It was a high, warbled, "Treeee treeee."

"Girls girls, come and look," I called. "Up there in the mountain ash tree! Look, it's a whole flock of birds."

There on our mountain ash tree was an entire flock of lovely, cream-colored birds. They sported cocky little feather points, at the back of their heads, and grey wings with a tiny crimson stripe near the base. These birds were busy. They were fluttering all over our tree and eating berries with gusto.

"What are they?" Crystal asked.

"I don't know," I replied.

We opened the door so that we could listen to their high-pitched call.

"There are hundreds of them," Crystal said.

"They're really gulping them down," Melody added with a grimace.

"Where's our bird book?" I asked and one of the girls went running for it.

We soon discovered that they were cedar waxwings. The robin-sized birds were gorging on the frozen mountain ash berries. They just kept grabbing them, tipping their heads backwards, and rolling them "down the hatch!" We watched and laughed at the greedy little birds for a while and then went back to other things.

About an hour later, I heard a bonk on one of the sunroom windows and noticed a stunned cedar waxwing sitting in the garden. *That isn't good,* I thought. *The barn cats will have a feast of him.* I quickly slipped on my shoes, headed outside, and picked him up, He seemed quite fine, except he strangely showed no fear. It almost seemed like he was grinning at me. I decided that the best thing for me to do would be to take him and set him into a spare bird cage for a bit until he was feeling better and could fly away from the cats.

"Melody, look!" I said, holding out the bird to her. "We've got a cedar waxwing here. He hit his head on the window. Could we put him in one of your extra cages?"

"Sure," she answered and ran to pull one out from where it was stored.

Melody, the little bird lover, was more than willing, she was excited. She gently took the bird from my hand and set him into a cage on some soft paper. "There you go, little one," she crooned. "You'll feel better soon."

After a couple of hours, I reached into the cage and picked him up once more. He was still a very demure and fearless little bird. I gently took him outside and tried tossing him into the air. He flapped a bit and landed on the branch of a fir tree. *Okay, he's probably safe,* I thought. But then, I saw another waxwing sitting on the grass and looking up at me. I called the girls and together we gently collected four or five birds. They were a good size and each bird more than filled our hands.

What could be wrong? I thought. "Are these birds sick, have they been poisoned?" I asked out loud, not expecting an answer.

The girls and I were very concerned and spent the next few hours checking in on them regularly. Suddenly, one little bird, seemed to burp, and up came a few berries. He burped again and up came a few more. I counted fifteen berries lying on the bottom of the cage before he began to flutter and let us know that he was ready to fly.

"I think that he is ready to be let loose," I commented, shaking my head in thought.

Melody opened the cage door and reached in to pick him up. He was still very calm, and didn't struggle. We took him outside and she gently tossed him into the air. He flapped his wings a bit and was gone. The other waxwings were beginning to look more chipper as well, so we managed to let each of them out of the cage and watched them fly into nearby trees. One or two birds didn't pass the test of flapping their wings and flying up to safety, but landed on the grass once more with an almost comical grin on their beaks.

"Back to the cage," I said, "or else the cats will make a nice meal out of you." Eventually, the last little birds were able to be released to safety.

When Dad arrived home, the girls were all excited to tell him about their interesting day.

"These birds were all just gulping our berries," Melody told him, and then they couldn't fly and landed on the ground, and we put them into cages and eventually they could fly again and what do you think is happening?"

"I don't know," he said, shaking his head. "Maybe we'll find out tomorrow."

The next day the flock had returned and was noisily gulping down frozen berries. An hour later, we had a group of waxwings sitting calmly on the ground and looking up at us with pleasant confidence. We picked them up and brought them to safety. A couple of hours later, they were just fine and flew away. One waxwing, the first to recover, took to burping again and coughed up a dozen ripe mountain ash berries.

I began to smell a rat. Were these relaxed and passive birds actually drunks that had been on a berry binge? Before releasing the burpy one, I asked Melody to find me a felt marker. I blackened the little guy's leg above his ankle and told the girls that we would watch for him tomorrow because I thought that he was a repeat offender.

Sure enough, before the following morning was over, our little waxwing lush was as pickled as could be. He was practically asking to be let into the Belcher-family drunk tank once more. We obliged and then released our happy drunk along with his friends when they sobered up.

The mountain ash tree was almost empty of the bright-red berries that these birds found so delicious. The next day only a few waxwings flew around the tree for a very short period and then left. These little birds certainly didn't know how to control their appetites. I hoped that the next farm with a mountain ash tree also had a drunk tank.

Every athlete exercises self-control in all things.
1Co 9:25 ESV

THE REAL TAILS OF EASY YOKE FARM

Pickled Waxwing.

Poor Hairy

There he was, perched on my sundeck—a pretty, hairy woodpecker. He had black feathers on the top of his little head and a bright-red patch on the back of his head. His chest was white and his wings were black with white spots. He was a very handsome little fellow.

Why wasn't he perched on a tree using his sharp, long beak to poke for bugs? Why wasn't he banging his beak on something to make the loud rat-tat-tat noise that woodpeckers make? This woodpecker was sitting in front of my cat's dinner dish…a very dangerous place to sit! I peeked through the kitchen curtain at this lovely little bird. I knew that he was called a hairy woodpecker because of the tiny feathers at the top of his beak and on his legs. Then I noticed that Hairy had a very big problem. His whole upper beak had been broken off. Only his bottom beak was still there. I felt very sad. Without his top beak Hairy couldn't drill holes in the trees to poke around for bugs. Hairy would get so hungry that he would die. Poor Hairy.

That wasn't Hairy's only problem. My cat would soon come home for breakfast. I didn't want him to find an extra bird treat in his bowl. As I watched, I realized that God had made Hairy a very brave and smart woodpecker. Hairy was already having his own dinner. He was scooping up Whiskas cat food with his bottom beak, tossing it into the air, and catching it with his open mouth. Hairy was eating cat food and looked like he was enjoying it.

Hairy had a good breakfast and flew away. The next day he showed up again and flipped piece upon piece of cat food into the air and caught it in his mouth. He never missed. All winter long, Hairy ate cat food; lots and lots of cat food. He ate so much cat food that I was sure that he would begin to "Meow!" Soon I noticed a wonderful thing happening. God was truly taking care of this brave little woodpecker. Hairy's top beak was getting longer. God was helping it to grow back.

By springtime, Hairy had a new top beak. It was a little crooked, but I noticed that Hairy was eating less Whiskas and coming for dinner less often. God had kept Hairy safe and fat all winter long, and now he could do all the things that woodpeckers like to do.

In the Bible, God tells us that He knows when each sparrow falls. He also knew when little Hairy broke his beak and gave him the bravery to come and enjoy dinner in a very strange place. Hairy spent the winter dining in his enemy's food dish. God also loves us and wants to care for us. We can be sure that God cares for us even more than He cared for Hairy.

Thou preparest a table before me in the presence of mine enemies. Psalm 23: 5

Goats in Coats: Well, at Least Sweatshirts!

It wasn't long before winter arrived with a vengeance. We discovered that our farm sat on a frigid corner. Icy winds shrieked up the creek from the lake, roared down a hill behind us called Frozen John, and raced in snowy, whiteout billows along the highway. In an act of pity, the previous owner dropped over to show us city folks how to put up the snow fence. We were grateful.

The blowing snow kept piling up and burying us in and the long driveway that widened out enough for numerous cars and trucks to park in it needed daily plowing. We were thankful that a small John Deere tractor had been part of our sale agreement. Thomas seemed to enjoy the role of gentleman farmer, even if his bundled up, snow-covered form resembled the abominable snowman with a totally frozen beard and icicled moustache. The plowing and shovelling of that driveway and the walkways on the farm was a brutal chore, but we all took turns and then thawed out in our blessed hot tub.

THE REAL TAILS OF EASY YOKE FARM

Inside, the house was warm and cozy with gas heat, a small but effective wood stove in the basement, and the huge living room fireplace.

Christmas passed but we never forgot that something very important was still missing. Our lovely red barn was still empty.

We had promised our girls that they could choose an animal that they really wanted. It was no secret that Melody wanted a little horse and Crystal wanted sheep. We began to look around for just the right animals for each of them.

Meanwhile, I came across an ad in a newspaper offering goats for sale. I discussed it with Thomas. Thomas and I thought that goats would be a good start to our herd. He'd had goats as a child. They give milk, and you could learn to make cheese.

"I found an ad in the newspaper that said that a lady is selling some milk goats that are expecting kids," I said one morning. "What would you think about starting our farm with a couple of milk goats?"

"Sure, yeah, that would be great," came the replies from around the breakfast table.

"When could we go and get them?" Melody asked.

"Should I give the lady a call?" I asked, turning to my husband.

"Why not?" he replied, and I headed to the phone and dialed.

"I read an ad that said that you had a couple of milk goats for sale," I said to the lady who answered.

"That's right," answered the lady. "They're due to have their kids in April."

"Can we come out and see them?"

"Sure," she replied and she gave me some vague country directions.

We decided that we would head out the following Saturday and all waited anxiously for the big day to arrive.

Before long, it was time for us to go and pick up our nanny goats and we all excitedly set out. It was very cold outside; minus thirty and snowing hard. Every one of us was completely bundled up with down parkas, gloves, scarves, and winter boots. Still, with the van heat on full blast we the city folks were all shivering with cold. We followed the lady's vague country directions and it seemed as though we were travelling forever. Eventually, after a few hours, we found the farm and carefully made our way through ruts and snow piles into a small barnyard.

"Are you sure that this is it?" Crystal asked, wide eyed.

Before us were lights draped over a rough wooden structure, and the goat sheds were simply tarps over hay bales. Many goats were lounging and eating under the tarps and didn't seem really bothered by the cold. The farmer's wife saw us through the window and came out to meet us.

Thomas raised his hand as a small woman in a well-worn barn parka approached.

"I'm Thomas Belcher, this is my wife, Rosemary, my sons Paul and David, and my daughters Crystal and Melody."

The lady looked us over good. I guessed that she wanted to make sure that her nannies were going to a good home.

I'm sure that she could tell that we were city folks. But finally she went into the lighted shelter with us trailing behind her. She looked around carefully and then stopped by a pair of lounging nannies and introduced us to two, lovely, tall, white Saanen goats.

"This is Rachel, and this is her sister Leah," she said warmly as she hooked up their leads. "Rachel has the pink collar, and Leah has the blue collar."

We all thought that it was interesting that the two goat sisters had names that matched the two sisters who became the wives of Jacob, the patriarch in the Bible. The lady handed their leads to Crystal and Melody.

" Hi baby, I'm Melody," Melody crooned to Leah.

"And I'm Crystal," Crystal said to Rachel as she rubbed Rachel's long goat neck up and down.

Every spare hand began patting the two new ladies, who stood calmly as we paid for them and headed back to the car.

None of us, with the exception of Thomas, had ever seen a goat close up, let alone led one, or requested that it jump into a van. These goats seemed quite happy to leave with us and willingly jumped in. After closing the van door to near-blizzard conditions, we tackled the long, two-hour trip home, with the goats squeezed into the foot spaces between the seats. The kids petted and talked to our new family members all the way home, and both goats seemed to be quite friendly and pleased to come along for the ride.

When we reached the farm, we led the goats into the barnyard and then into the lovely, little red barn where clean hay stalls and lots of fresh hay abounded.

I saw the frost on the inside of the barn roof, and was worried about our new charges. "Are you sure that they are going to be warm enough?" I asked Thomas with deep concern.

"Do you remember where these two came from? They didn't have any real shelter at all from the cold, only bales to keep the worst of the wind off. This is going to be heaven compared to where they came from," Thomas reminded me.

Regardless, I worried about our two goats all night long. At some point in the wee dark hours, I got a brainwave and with morning light, went up to see the girls. "Girls do you have a couple of sweatshirts that you would give to Rachel and Leah to help keep them warm?" I pleaded.

It didn't take much and within minutes we were slogging through the deep snow towards the barn to try them on.

Melody put the salmon one on Rachel, and Leah wore Crystal's baby-blue one. The goats seemed quite pleased and were also very pleased with the nice feed that we put into their dinner trays. These two would not be giving us milk until they had had their new kids, so we left the barn door open and released our fashionable goats into the barnyard, where they jumped all over hay bales and ran around in glee and satisfaction. We had a few neighbours honk and laugh when they saw our sweatshirt-wearing goats running around the pastures, but this was nothing. There was more to come.

THE REAL TAILS OF EASY YOKE FARM

Morning chores in the barnyard began that day by feeding and watering Rachel and Leah. Our family did have other morning routines, though. The girls or I would take care of breakfast, two others would head to the barnyard for feeding and watering animals, and the others would get the tractor and begin plowing the driveway and snow shoveling the sidewalks beside the house and the path to the barn as well as the stile steps.

By seven, we all sat down to breakfast and then gathered together in the sunroom or living room where a passage from the Bible was read. Then the family prayed together and asked the Lord to bless our day and bring us all safely home again together that evening.

By eight, the family had scattered to their various day activities and the kitchen crew tidied up breakfast dishes and made their beds, etc.

Now, at some point, we expected that spring would appear, although it sure was slower than happened down south.

One day we received a call from a farmer. "Hello, my name is Jake, and I had a ewe, (a momma sheep) die during the night when she gave birth. There are twin lambs, and without someone to bottle feed them they will certainly die. I heard that you have a couple of girls. Would one of them like to have them?"

Well, I looked at Crystal, who couldn't hear the conversation, and asked,

"Would you like a couple of lambs?"

Crystal jumped with glee. "Yes!" she cried. Her dream was finally coming true.

That afternoon, the farmer brought us two, oatmeal-colored, adorable lambs with black faces.

"I'm going to name them Keviss and Kivsah," Crystal announced. These were Hebrew names that basically meant little ram and little ewe. We scrounged some lamb bottles and bought some lamb milk replacer, and the two little lambs enjoyed their first feeding. Crystal could hardly hold onto the bottles, they tugged so hard. Their little tails wagged with joy. They bleated and she learned to copy their bleat and talk back to them.

After their feeding, Crystal put them on little leashes and like Bo Peep herself walked them proudly around the barnyard while they leapt and gamboled and played. Every few hours she filled those warm bottles in the kitchen. Then she stood out on the back porch for just a moment and let out the most convincing "Baaaa" that you have ever heard from human lips. "Baaaaaa. Baaaaaaaa."

From the barnyard echoed the joyful bleatings of two ecstatic little lambs. They leapt up on the fence with their tails wagging with joy awaiting their mommy to come and feed them. Soon, our two goats and the lambs played and ran together and the pastures began to come alive.

There were still missing but not forgotten promises. Melody was patiently waiting and praying for a little horse. Finally, we heard of a little seven-month-old palomino, for sale. I was pleased because a palomino is a very pretty, tan-colored horse with a white mane and white tail. I could imagine such a lovely horse out grazing with the other animals.

THE REAL TAILS OF EASY YOKE FARM

"I think that we might have found you a horse, Melody," I said.

She grinned a huge grin and jiggled up and down for joy.

"Now this might not be the one, so don't get your hopes up too high, okay?" I cautioned.

"Okay," she answered, but being her mother, I was sure that all the while she was hoping that this was the one.

I made a call to the farmer, and we headed out to the farm. The little horse was adorable, beautiful, and absolutely everything that Melody could have dreamed about. She gently patted his neck and looked at us with pleading eyes.

We forked over the price of one promised little horse and immediately she named him Prince.

Prince was delivered that very afternoon to a very excited girl. She proudly led him to the barn. She brushed him and fed him and loved on him and found it very hard to leave him at suppertime. He wasn't very big, and of course we had no idea about how to care for a horse. We knew that they needed brushing, and feeding and clean water and a nice clean stall to sleep in. That's all, right?

Melody took good care of him, but when I went out into the barnyard to care for the goats, Prince would come up and nudge and push a bit because he knew that my barn jacket pockets were full of the alfalfa crunchies that I fed to the goats.

So, I would give in to the adorable little horse and give him a crunchy just to get him to leave me alone long enough to bring in a few square bales of hay. Prince wasn't going to leave me alone. He was a little stinker that wasn't so little and was growing fast. He was also teething. Prince was making my barn chores very frustrating in the mornings because he was getting more and more pushy. He even began to nip at my pockets and hands to convince me to pay attention to him.

I began to carry an old broom stick with me. No, not to hit the little horse. As I said, he was teething and as long as he could grab onto the broomstick and walk along beside me, he was perfectly happy. So, Prince and I did all the barn chores that were on my watch as a couple. I used my left hand as much as possible with Prince chomping on the broomstick that I held in the other.

Horse people are probably shaking their heads in amazement here, but we were city folks and just didn't know. Our animals did great, though, and the little horse grew bigger and stronger and gave Melody hours of delight.

As spring sprung, our barnyard wasn't empty any more. A sassy little palomino along with two of the cutest lambs, two wonderful patient milk goats, and a whole barn loft full of every color of kitty that you could imagine brought life and joy into the lives of these city folks, who were beginning to become farmers. Now we had to learn how to care for them.

Be thou diligent to know the state of thy flocks, and look well to thy herds. Pr 27:23

THE REAL TAILS OF EASY YOKE FARM

Crystal and her lambs.

ROSEMARY RONNLUND BELCHER

Leah, a true lady. Photo Credit: Brechin Mclaine

Buttercup's Special Friend

Long before we moved to our little farm, we knew that we needed to buy a cow. We wanted a nice friendly cow that would give lots of nice sweet milk. We thought about having fresh cream, butter, and maybe trying to make our own cheese. We asked around and finally found a farmer who was willing to sell a good, gentle, milk cow.

One afternoon, a pickup truck pulling a horse trailer drove down the long farm driveway and parked in front of the pasture gates. The farmer went to the rear of his trailer, put down the ramp, and walked a very big brown cow over to me. Of course, I was from the city, and even though I love animals, I'd never even been close to a cow, let alone a huge cow like this one. He handed me the rope, said, "Her name is Buttercup," climbed into the cab of his truck, and away he went.

I stood there holding the lead and wondering what to do. I looked into her huge brown eyes and finally said, "Come on, sweetheart." I gave a little tug on the rope and she nicely followed me inside the pasture gate where I let her loose to enjoy some fresh, green grass. As she walked away,

I couldn't help but notice that very large udder swaying beneath her and knew that we all were going to have to learn to milk.

That evening, at milking time, Thomas and I, Crystal, and Paul sat on both sides of Buttercup on tall, upturned white buckets. Melody and David stood behind us and watched closely. We each took one warm, wrinkly teat in our hands and wiggled and twisted it until we learned how to get a nice stream of fresh milk to spray into the milk bucket that we had placed underneath her.

"Hey quit it!" David complained as a squirt of sticky warm milk shot up onto his shirt. Crystal then shot and hit Paul, and then Dad and I joined in. The girls squealed as they became targets and although Buttercup was patient, she had to know that there was a jolly Belcher family war taking place right beneath her. I have to admit that it took about two hours before the bucket was full, and patient Buttercup stood just as nice as could be the whole time. She was definitely the cow that we had prayed for.

The next morning, when we sat down to milk, we realized that we had learned a lot the evening before and the pail filled much quicker with only two of us doing the milking. We had gotten over the urge to squirt milk at each other, but the barn cats enjoyed some warm streams that were aimed towards them. It was cute to see their little pink tongues lapping as fast as they could while milk dribbled all over their whiskers and down their fur. They didn't mind a bit.

THE REAL TAILS OF EASY YOKE FARM

That afternoon, as Buttercup grazed happily in the pasture, the phone rang. It was the farmer who had sold Buttercup to us. He sounded very unhappy. "Hi, how are you doing? This is Joe here. How's Buttercup doing? I have a little situation here," he continued. "Buttercup has always been pastured with this sheep. They were best buddies. This sheep is going crazy without her cow. She's tearing around the pasture in a panic and looking for ways to escape. "Would you please take the sheep?" he begged.

Thomas and I looked at each other. He shrugged a thoughtful, *Why not?*

"Okay, I guess so," I answered. After all, how much trouble could one sheep be?

Within the hour, the horse trailer pulled in once more and a big woolly sheep was unloaded and put into our pasture. She saw Buttercup and tore across the field so fast she actually stumbled a couple of times. When the sheep reached her cow, Buttercup seemed to arch her back. Then the sheep, whose name was Felice, shoved her way underneath her. Buttercup went back to eating and her four-legged belly warmer contentedly began eating as well. Across the pasture they munched, travelling like a double decker bus.

Later on, when the excitement was over, Felice came out of hiding and grazed beside the large cow for a while, but hurried back under if she felt threatened.

The season changed to golden trees, and then winter snow. We watched with amazement every day as Buttercup arched her back to let a snow-covered friend hide beneath her warmth. It was easy to see that Buttercup struggled with the icy chill, though her friendship was more important to her than a chilly tummy.

But Buttercup also got to enjoy the benefits of friendship. Buttercup usually had a damp cow nose that seemed to be forever itchy, and so whenever she liked she could just reach down and rub it on the fluffy back of her best friend. I hope that I am as patient and loving towards my friends as Buttercup and Felice, the fluffy sheep, are to each other

Love one another. John 15:17

Buttercup with her nose in Felice's wool.

The Fawn and the Kitty

One cool spring morning as I was driving with a tiny grandson who was wiggling in his car seat, I noticed something special. A tiny new fawn lay in the shade of a small tree. It was curled up in a little ball, and the small white spots on its back looked just like tiny white flowers. The little fawn lay just where its mommy had left it. Mother deer often leave their little ones to nap and go off for a quiet dinner. God has given little deer those tiny white spots to camouflage them so that they won't be noticed by other animals or people that could hurt them.

"Look Sammy," I whispered, rolling down the car window as quietly as possible. "Shhh." I held my finger up to my lips to let him know that we had to be very quiet. "Look at the baby deer, he still has his baby spots. He's over there lying in the grass."

Sammy took a moment to find what I was showing him and broke into a big grin.

"Shhh." I smiled and warned him again.

In the next yard, we could see Mommy Deer calmly eating fresh grass. She must have told the little fawn something like this: *You lie down here and have a nice nap and Mommy will go over to the next yard and have some breakfast.*

"Oh, look," I whispered excitedly. "Someone else is coming!"

It wasn't a big dog, or even a person. Through the long grass tiptoed

a little gray kitty. The little fawn wasn't alone anymore.

The kitty peeked around the small tree, and took a good look at the little fawn. Closer and closer it came. The little fawn looked up wide eyed. I imagine it had never seen a little kitty. The kitty stretched its neck towards the little fawn and the little fawn stretched its long neck towards the little kitty. They touched noses! Both of them jumped and pulled their heads back.

Very carefully they stretched out and touched noses again, and this time they had a very good sniff. The little kitty happily bounced backwards and the little fawn forgot what his mother had told him about hiding quietly and taking a nap and stood up on his wobbly legs. The kitty took a few leaps through the tall grass.

"Watch what they're doing," I encouraged my little grandson.

Little fawn took a few wobbly leaps through the tall grass. Little kitty bounded to the edge of the grass. Little fawn bounded to the edge of the grass. Suddenly, little kitty bounded across the road. Little fawn took a few wobbly but joyful leaps across the road after her and followed the kitty into another yard.

Oh dear, I thought to myself. There was Mommy Deer happily grazing on one side of the road and the little fawn was chasing a kitty on the other side. The little fawn wasn't safe anymore. Big dogs could chase him, cars could run over him, and he could get lost. He was in danger because he had forgotten to obey.

"That little fawn has forgotten to obey his mommy," I said sadly. "I hope that she will be able to find him when she comes back."

Sammy looked at the little fawn and the tiny grey kitty happily playing together. He was too small to really understand, but those of you who are reading probably feel worried for the fawn, just like I did.

Have you ever disobeyed Mom or Dad by doing what you wanted to do instead of what they told you to do? God gives us moms and dads to protect us and teach us to do what is right. God tells us this in His word, the Bible. When we obey our parents, we please God.

What happened to the little fawn? Well, later in the day when I was driving Sammy home, we saw Mommy Deer and the fawn lying together in a garden. So I guess that she found him just fine. I'm sure, though, that Mommy Deer was going to make sure that Little Fawn learned to obey. I never did see him running off again!

Children, obey your parents in the Lord:
for this is right. Ephesians 6:1

ROSEMARY RONNLUND BELCHER

Sammy helps out.

Blossom is Born

Buttercup, our cow, spent her days grazing out in the pastures along with her special friend Felice, the sheep. Felice was her favorite companion, but Buttercup had a secret. Her cow tummy was growing bigger and bigger, and it wasn't because she was eating too much grain and fresh grass. Buttercup was getting ready to have a calf. We were all very excited.

We all watched the weather and hoped that it would warm up. Leah and Rachel, our nanny goats, were also going to have their babies around the same time. As a city person, I had no idea how to deal with animal births, so I decided that we would continue to give them lots of loving care and call the vet if we needed her.

The winter flew by so quickly. There were sundogs, and ice crystal pillars standing in the fields. There were amazing night auroras. The Northern Lights, were so spectacular that we all had to climb into the van and head for the nearest truly dark spot a few miles north. There we could really enjoy them in all their glory. We were awestruck by the twirling green and pink pinwheels and the swooping fingers of colors that crossed the sky and then dropped down in majesty to almost touch the earth. Our whole family, who loves to sing, literally broke out in harmonious song and sang praises to the Lord, who made everything and bought us to this beautiful land and life.

When the snow began to melt, my barnyard ladies' tummies were getting bigger and bigger, and I could often see moving bulges in all of them. This was both scary and exciting. I had grown close to all of the animals and especially Buttercup and the nanny goats.

One day, I noticed that Buttercup was lying on some clean straw and her tummy seemed to be moving in rhythmic motions. *She's having her baby*, I thought with excitement. All of our kids were off at school or work and even my dear hubby wasn't there. *What do I do? ...I would want some comfort,* I thought so I lay down on the hay beside her with my head softly on her busy tummy and begin to sing all the pretty songs that I felt she might enjoy. I sang nursery rhymes about the cow that jumped over the moon, and Old McDonald's farm; singing the moo moo here, and a moo moo there quite a few times.

I had heard that cows sometimes needed their babies pulled out with chains because they get stuck, but surely a cow that is calm and happy could have her calf gently and in peace. The contractions continued. Buttercup raised her head and began panting and letting out little groans.

I went to stand up but she looked at me and groaned in protest so I lay down once again. Looking behind me, I noticed a big dark bubble that was emerging from her special baby place under her tail. Inside the bubble wiggled two sizeable hooves. I moved behind Buttercup so that I could watch more closely, but I kept singing. I was running out of new songs so I had to keep singing the same ones over and over again. Buttercup didn't seem to mind at all. She continued to give little grunts and pushes and more of a little calf appeared. Pretty soon the calf was nearly all out with the exception of its back legs. So, I gently grabbed baby and gave a little tug. The calf slipped out easily.

Buttercup turned her head around and then stood up and began licking her baby to help it to breathe better. I still sat right behind her back legs, but she seemed happy to have me, her birthing companion, there. In minutes the little calf stood up and began searching for a nipple to nurse from. I let baby nurse and then ran for the scales. Buttercup mooed after me until I returned.

I struggled to hang the little one in the scales and found that she was only eighty pounds. *Oh oh,* I thought. *This calf is too small.* Cows are big animals and I thought that surely their calves would be a lot heavier than this. *What do I do?* But I found out later that eighty pounds is a perfect weight for a calf.

I was so excited and thankful to the Lord that He not only could cover the night sky with amazing beauty, but knew just how to help our momma cow safely give birth. My heart filled with praise as I watched the little calf. When I saw that she was a female and looked around at the beautiful blossoms on the spring trees, I knew just what to name her: "Blossom."

ROSEMARY RONNLUND BELCHER

Let them praise the name of the LORD:
for his name alone is excellent;
his glory is above the earth and heaven. Psalm 148:13

Young Blossom lounging in her sun hat.

Punkin, Punkin, Punkin

The farm was a whirr with new babies, more chores, seeds to plant, and many other new tasks that we city dwellers had never even thought of.

One sunny Saturday morning, when we all seemed to be outside, a small car rumbled down the driveway. Crystal had her arms full of kittens, and Melody had picked up a contented hen. She had placed it on her head like a hat and was waltzing around with a *look at me* grin.

I had just crossed over the stile from the barnyard and the guys were doing yard chores and repairs. We all gathered to see who was coming for a visit.

The car door opened and a tiny, elderly woman climbed out. Reaching onto the seat beside her, she soon held a wiggly little bundle in her arms. Looking carefully over the bunch of us, she quickly approached Melody and firmly placed the bundle in her arms.

The girls' eyes widened. "Awwwww," came their drawn-out response. The wiggly bundle was a chubby chocolate lab pup. Crystal immediately set the kittens down. Melody plucked the contented hen off of her head with her free arm and hugged the squirming pup with both arms. Crystal joined in the hugging, and both girls began crooning:

"Oh, you're so cute."

"You're such a sweet puppy."

"Oh look, Mom. She's so adorable."

What we basically missed until we heard her voice was that the spry, elderly lady had hightailed it to her little car. As she climbed in she called, "I have things to do. I'll be back at four to find out if you want it!"

With that she boogied like a race car driver down the long driveway and was gone.

Well, it was close to ten in the morning and four o'clock seemed like a long way away when your girls were already ogling and cuddling an adorable puppy.

"Can we keep her?"

"Can we, Mom?"

"Oh, Daddy look! She's so cute. We could use another dog. Candy is getting old."

"She's so cute."

"Please, Daddy. Please!"

I can't remember who was pleading and begging with what words, but the boys appeared, and they too soon had their loving hands all over that squirmy pup. Melody suddenly turned her back to everyone, just to keep her prize to herself. And she did think that it was her prize and her puppy. After all, whose arms did it get put into?

"Just wait a minute," Dad cautioned. "We have to think about this."

He looked at me. We both knew that we had been bamboozled by a sharp elderly lady, who could boogie away in her little car like no other.

"Can you believe this?" I asked Thomas with wide eyes, which kept turning to peek at the adorable pup.

"She's got some nerve!" he commented, though he couldn't help but grin. "I wouldn't think that an elderly lady could plan something like this and carry it out!"

I agreed, shaking my head in amused unbelief at her bravery and skill. "Candy *is* getting old," I said. "She's getting blind, and those coyotes come pretty close to our chickens each night. She could use some backup."

"But who's going to take care of it?" Dad questioned.

The answer came swiftly. "I will! I will!" Melody cried.

"Me too!" Crystal added, jubilantly sensing a win.

"But she's my puppy!" Melody said firmly, turning once more to shield her pup from the other hands that reached out to it.

"He's not all yours!" Crystal argued.

"She gave him to me!" came the firm and almost angry statement from a usually calm young girl.

"He belongs to all of us!" the boys commented firmly.

We surveyed our ruffled offspring, who were all laying claim to one small pup. Then Dad's eyes fell onto his youngest, whose arms not only cradled the small pup but held it under her neck. She had her elbow out as if she was ready to defend herself and her charge from anyone who might try to take it away from her.

"Do you promise to take good care of him, Melody?" Dad asked with raised eyebrows.

"Yes, yes, I promise, I promise!" she cried jumping up and down with glee.

"He's going to have to be housebroken," I added. "You'll be the one cleaning up all the messes and accidents."

"Yeah, in our bedroom!" Crystal almost sneered. She was the fastidious girl who demanded that everything be squeaky clean. "And it better be good and smell good too!" she added in frustration

"I know, I know!" Melody assured us in a pleading tone. "I'll take care of everything!"

"Okay then," Dad said nodding his head thoughtfully. "Remember, it's your responsibility!"

"I know, I promise," Melody replied solemnly, and then with a grin she disappeared with her treasure into the house and up to the girls' room. A few minutes later she appeared with the pup, who now had a long pink hair ribbon tied to her collar.

"I'm going to call her Punkin," Melody announced.

Crystal headed back out to the barnyard to be with her lambs. Even though the responsibility had become Melody's, there would always be lots of Punkin to go around.

Lunch passed, and when four o'clock chimed, the elderly lady reappeared once more in a cloud of dust, got out and said, "Well?"

"We want her, we want her!" the kids, especially the girls, chorused.

"Good," the lady responded with firmness. "This was the biggest and the naughtiest puppy in the litter! I'm glad that she's found a good home."

With that, she rumbled down the driveway and was gone in a cloud of dust.

Punkin was a handful! She climbed all over the aging Candy and chewed her ears. She chewed appliance cords, furniture legs, socks, and stuffed toys, she basically chewed everything that she could sink her needle-like teeth into. Yet she wiggled and squirmed her way into every heart.

I just loved her. She had that new-puppy smell. Now, human babies seem to have a new-baby smell, that is when they don't need changing. New puppies in my opinion smell like mushroom soup. I just love the smell of a cuddly new pup, and Punkin was definitely cuddly. She slept with Melody and often snuck over to sleep with Crystal, and all was well.

Punkin actually housetrained pretty easily, and I can't remember too many accidents. But I did blame her for one crime that she was completely innocent of.

We had purchased some nice geese to raise and were looking forward to roast goose.

I read all the recipes that I could find and tried to figure out the best way to roast my goose. On the appointed day, the girls and I took the prepared goose from my husband and got it ready for the roaster.

Melody loved to make bread and buns and got her dough rising pretty much right after breakfast so she could bake her buns before the goose had to go into the oven.

"I get to use the oven first, for my cake," Crystal stated.

"That will be fine," I assured her, "because Melody's yeast buns still have to rise."

Crystal made her cake into a delectable dessert. She was a wonderful baker. I prepared veggies and kept a close eye on the goose.

At dinner time the whole family had their mouths watering and we sat up to the table with great anticipation. Punkin, meanwhile, had managed to keep her nose clean throughout the meal preparation. She had been babysat by poor old Candy, who let Punkin follow her throughout the farmyard and sniff all of the animals who lived there.

The table was beautifully set by the girls, the food was going into serving dishes, and I was attempting my first goose carving. Well, I thought it should be just like carving a turkey, and I began my attack with a carving knife.

The goose was greasy. It oozed grease and although I had seasoned it nicely, I had to pretty much shake off the grease before putting each piece on the serving platter. It didn't smell great either.

Dinner was okay, but disappointing. Usually two people cleaned up the dishes each night. Not wanting to be wasteful, I decided that surely I could put the bones and leftover meat (after laying it onto paper towel) into the crockpot and at least we could have goose soup tomorrow.

I carefully put the remaining goose into the crockpot along with some onions and carrots. I thought that maybe I could redeem the goose and we could find a way to enjoy it.

THE REAL TAILS OF EASY YOKE FARM

By bedtime the goose was simmering safely, and the farm became quiet, with the exception of the night journeys of the coyote family as they scouted out our locked chicken coop.

In the wee hours, I woke up. Something was not right. There was a terrible smell. I got up. It smelled like the dog had had an accident somewhere, and I knew that faithful old Candy would not be the guilty party. I carefully stepped out of bed and onto the chilly floor. I was sure that at any time my toes were going to be swallowed by a smelly pile of doggy doo. Boy, Melody was going to hear about this in the morning! She was supposed to keep Punkin shut up with them in their room, so that if the dog had to go that she could take her outside. Obviously Punkin, that sneaky little bundle of trouble, had already snuck out and found a place to relieve herself. Then she'd snuck back to bed with the girls unnoticed.

I began cautiously tiptoeing around the house. The poo wasn't in our bedroom, thank heavens. I tiptoed through the living room and my nose told me that this room was not soiled either. Was it the sunroom? I wandered onwards.

The sunroom was filled with glorious moonlight. The yard was more than beautiful, with long shadows and branches and flowers coated in shimmering light. The poo smell was increasing as I roamed past the hot tub room, along the big windows, past the birdcages, and turned into the kitchen.

I had found the room! It was here, I knew it! The dog had snuck down and gone in the kitchen, for sure. Now maybe that meant that the poor pup was really trying to let itself outside, but just hadn't made it. *I may have to be a little lenient*, I thought.

My nose led me onwards towards the oven and then towards the kitchen island, but the floor was clean. The smell, however, was terrible.

I raised my head, and homed in on my very own crock-pot. My goose was cooked!

That was the last goose that we tried to eat. They made a pretty addition to the little pond that Thomas and the boys had dug, which was surrounded with Crystal's perennials, The geese honked, waddled, and floated there throughout the summer and then were sold to another farm with few regrets. Punkin was not the culprit, Melody was off the hook, and farm life with a little bundle of busy continued.

Now, I said that she chewed. Punkin was the biggest babysitting project ever. When the family was up and busy, she would run up to one person to check out what they were doing and then go on to the next. But when we sat down for family time and we were trying to be still, the little pup just couldn't handle it.

Our family had a special time each morning. We shared our prayer requests and then each of us prayed. It was a peaceful and comforting few minutes as we got ready to face our various days. Punkin squirmed from one lap to the other and finally we decided to put her on the floor and let her roam just for a moment's peace. We did get peace. Then I shuddered knowing that a very quiet puppy, just like a child, may be busy doing something that they shouldn't.

We finished our quiet time and went to search for the little monster and found her quite content. She had discovered the little arch pads in everyone's shoes and runners and found them to be quite tasty. They had all disappeared, apart from some bits and chewings that were all over the kitchen floor. We all groaned. I was going to have to shop for insoles for everyone's shoes because buying six new pairs of shoes was out of the question. Would she ever grow up? "Oh, Punkin, Punkin Punkin!"

Love is patient. Love is kind. 1Co 13:4

The Grateful Swallow

One early-spring morning, a long line of little birds sat twittering on a wire. The snow was still on the ground, but as the snow melted, the birds happily dove and swooped as they feasted on all the new spring bugs.

That afternoon, my husband came home with something clasped in his hand. "Look what I brought you," he said with a smile. There in his hand was a tiny swallow. He told me that a neighbour had cleaned out his gutters and knocked a nest onto the ground.

"I thought that I should bring it to you to take care of before a cat found it," he said.

I gently took the tiny creature from his hand. "This little bird eats insects," I told him sadly. "It doesn't eat seeds like the little finches that we used to have."

The tiny bird looked up at me with trusting eyes. He opened his little mouth and hoped that I would feed him. I sighed and held him up to my shirt to see if his little feet would want to grab on and he opened his tiny claws and clung happily like a little brooch while I prayed about what I could do for this little creation of God.

THE REAL TAILS OF EASY YOKE FARM

Through the window I noticed that swallows were happily flitting about high in the air. Maybe if I set this little fellow in a place where his mom and dad could see him they would come and get him. Just outside the back door was a hanging basket that was growing nothing but grass.

I gently placed the little fellow on the grass and then gave him a few drops of water from an eye dropper. He drank it down joyfully. As the basket swung gently in the breeze, the tiny bird gazed skyward at his family flying overhead. He began squawking little baby squawks, and whenever I came to give him a little drink, I encouraged him to squawk louder. He squawked all afternoon but no birds came to visit. I continued to pray and ask God to send his parents to find him. .

As the sky darkened, I wondered what I should do. Would he be safe on the porch? If I took him inside, would his parents pay a visit and then give up if he wasn't there? I left him there with a prayer for safety, and he swung all night in the spring breezes.

The next morning, I found him perky but thirsty. His family was already flying high so I gave him a drink and told the hungry little bird to squawk with all his might.

Around noon something exciting happened. Two adult swallows landed on the porch rail beside the basket where the little fellow was squawking loudly. I was so happy to see them and watched from behind the kitchen curtain. The two adult birds seemed to have a discussion and then flew off. That made me unhappy.

Before too long the birds returned with two other birds. These two jumped up on the edge of the hanging basket and began a serious conversation with the little bird. They fed him, and then had him sit on the edge of the basket and flap his little wings. Whether he was ready or not, his only hope of being rescued was to learn how to fly. The parents tutored, and flapped and chatted and chirped. One parent after another would jump into the air and fly around and back to the basket to show him how it was done.

The little bird was not very excited about flying, but finally climbed up and sat on the very edge. Then he flapped his tiny wings and flew over to the porch rail.

I was sure that I could hear the parent birds cheering him on—I know I was cheering. Then the adults flew off the porch. They looked backward and watched the little swallow flap his wings and follow them off into the big sky. How exciting to watch that little family flying away. I was so thankful to the Lord for answering my prayers.

It wasn't too many days later that I noticed the whole flock flying away to their next stop, where they would stay until winter had come and gone again.

The next spring, I began looking to the sky; wondering when the little flock of swallows would appear once more. One morning, I heard a loud twittering and noticed the entire flock was balancing on the telephone wire in the lane behind our house. I headed out on the porch and said some welcoming hellos, to the little birds.

As I stood smiling, an amazing and wonderful thing happened. One little bird left the wire and flew towards me.

THE REAL TAILS OF EASY YOKE FARM

Is this my little bird? I thought with my heart racing. A tiny adult swallow flew right towards me. He flew within two feet of me and turned his little belly to me and poised his feet as though he wanted to land on my blouse; just where he had sat when he was a nestling.

I held my breath as he flapped closer and closer, just hanging in the air. I spoke softly to him as he hovered, and then he flew back to his flock. Was this his *Thank you*? Was this, *I remember that you cared for me*? Whatever it was, the little bird had remembered. With a little more bravery, this tiny wild creature would have been perching on my blouse where he had felt so safe the year before.

The story doesn't end here. The next spring, when the flock returned, my little swallow left the flock once more. This time he flew right around me on the porch as I watched with glee. Then he returned to his twittering family.

The third year, he took a little break from lunch in the air and came alone to perch on the wire. He sang me a little song as I talked to him.

The next year there was a forest fire miles from our home. The birds must have taken some detours around the fires and landed elsewhere. I didn't see any swallows that year.

This spring, a tiny, lone bird came and sat on the wire. I talked to him for a while and then he flew off. Was this my grateful swallow, coming year after year to say *Thank you*? I'd like to think that it was.

I know that a tiny bird taught me a lesson that I will never forget: How important it is to say, "Thank you." I know that our merciful Lord, who watches over every little bird and helped me to save this little one also loves to hear us say, "Thank You."

O give thanks unto the God of heaven: for his mercy [endureth] for ever. Ps 136:26

The Stork Strikes Again

Now I'm sure that everyone reading this has heard that a big bird called a stork brings babies in little bundles and drops them down the right chimneys to the new waiting parents. Farm children know that that isn't the way things happen.

Our farm didn't have storks, just some fat geese, a few busy hens, two miserable roosters, and some quickly growing little turkeys. We had to have our farm babies the natural way, which, of course, is the way that all babies are meant to be born. I mentioned before that the goat mommy's tummies were getting very big and round and I could tell that inside that special baby section in their bodies there was a lot of commotion going on.

Leah's goat tummy was especially big and very busy. I was sure that she was having twins. One morning, Leah waddled out to meet me as I climbed over the stile to feed and water the animals. Now for those of you that don't know what a stile is, I'll tell you, It is simply a little set of stairs that goes up one side of the fence and down the other side. For some reason the animals don't try to use it to escape and so it is much nicer than having to unlatch heavy pasture gates.

I had just come over the stile, and Leah came right up to me. She was bleating more than usual. She kept looking at me and then turning her head back to her tail. Then she looked at me again with eyes that asked me if I was getting her message.

"You're trying to tell me that you're going to have your baby today," I said to her happily. "Come with me and we'll get you into a nice clean stall with soft straw."

Leah willingly followed me into the barn. I scattered fresh straw down, filled a bucket of water and made sure that her dinner dish had lots of nice grain and molasses. She ate and drank and then lay down.

I turned to leave so that I could get the rest of my chores done and she bleated loudly, straining to stand up and then follow me to the stall door. She definitely wanted me to stay with her. I explained that I would be back as soon as I could and went to finish my chores to the sound of Leah loudly protesting in the background.

The rest of the family had already left for work and so I was on chore duty.

Square bales of hay needed to be thrown down from the barn loft and broken up and scattered into various feeders. Grain had to be mixed in a special recipe and served into each animal's dishes. Water had to be hauled in tall buckets from the water tank and poured into the barnyard bathtub so that the animals could get a drink. It took at least six heavy buckets to fill that tub. And of course, Buttercup was mooing to be milked. She had to have her udder washed down carefully with warm soapy water, and then dried carefully. After I'd milked her, the milk buckets had to be taken right into the house and filtered through a special paper sheet into clean milk jars. The jars were then quickly placed into the fridge to cool. Later, when the rich cream rose to the top of the milk it was separated and used for making butter and sometimes delicious cheesecake.

I finished my chores, looking in on Leah now and then, and about forty-five minutes later I returned to Leah's stall. She was watching and impatiently waiting for me. Both of us lay or sat down on the soft straw. I started to sing to her just like I had to Buttercup.

Leah had a song that she really liked. Actually, it was a favorite song for all the goats. How do I know? Well, I just do. Somehow, they just let you know. My goats knew how to smile! Anyway, I began to sing and sing, but when I changed songs, Leah began to bleat in an annoyed way and so "Bill Goggin's Goat" it was over and over and over.

Leah's tummy seemed to tighten and loosen in rhythm for a couple of hours and then she began to pant. A bubble began to emerge from her baby place and I could see two little hooves wiggling in the bubble just like when Blossom had been born. They wiggled so much that they broke through the sac and pretty soon a little white nose and head could be seen cuddled up tightly to the little legs. Soon, a long neck, then some shoulders, and a little goat tummy slipped out. And suddenly, a new goat kid wiggled on the straw.

Leah turned happily to say hi to her little one, and both of us could tell that this was a boy! We had our first little buck.

Leah wasn't finished. Her tummy began its squeezing once again and another bubble began to show with two more little wiggly hooves. This was exciting. A second little goat kid was quickly born. Soon it was struggling to stand and enjoy its first meal of warm momma's milk. We had two lovely twins: a male and a female. I named the male Isaac, and he became our first daddy goat. The little female was named Promise, because I was reminded of all the promises that God has kept for us.

That evening, as the whole family returned from work, we all gathered in the barn to congratulate Leah. We enjoyed watching her twins trying to play and climb on their wobbly little legs. Leah was a happy, healthy mom and we left her in the stall for a couple of days. After that she could return to the barnyard with the other goats and sheep.

Now Rachel was also getting ready to have her first kid. Her tummy wasn't quite as big, so we were all just waiting for the big day to come.

One morning as I came over the stile I heard loud bleating coming from the barn. It sounded very strange. It sounded like Rachel and another little kid goat.

Has she had her baby on her own? I wondered.

As I entered the barn, I had my answer.

She had kind of had her baby in the night. Rachel was standing there bleating angrily for someone to come and help her. A wiggly little goat, with a black and white nose that was already perfectly dry, was sticking out of her baby place and also complaining loudly. I had a two-headed goat. Both of them were frustrated!

I smiled to myself, got out my vet gloves, and reached inside Rachel a wee bit to see why this frustrated baby was not fully born. It certainly had a loud bleat.

I could feel that inside of Rachel, the big healthy new kid was a little bit stuck. Rachel had what was called a shoulder lock and needed someone to give the new kid a little turn. I needed to help to ease its shoulders out and allow it to slip onto the straw.

Rachel stood with an *it's about time* look on her muzzle. She let me give baby a gentle little twist and then help to finish the birth.

It didn't take long before the feisty baby was on its feet and nursing, and a relieved Rachel was nuzzling it. She was happy to have it beside her and not still stuck in her.

The little goat was so cute that I named her Precious. Precious with all of her personality and determination, would add to the excitement in the barnyard in ways that we couldn't even imagine. It was a good day to have a farm and I knew that all of us, including all the animals, were under the Lord's loving care.

Let everything that hath breath praise the LORD. Praise ye the LORD. Psalm 150:6

Happy Birthday

It was a special day! There was cake and there were treats and birthday hats. There was going to be a birthday party on the farm. Whose birthday was it? Well, it was the first birthday of Crystal's twin sheep, Keviss and Kivsah.

How do you throw a party for a sheep? Just the same way that you would have one for anyone else…with great excitement.

The girls had been talking and planning for days. Everything had to be really special and pictures had to be taken just like at any other birthday party.

The birthday cake had to be special too. It started out with a loaf of bread that was a bit stale and hard. At a party you want to serve food that your guests will want to eat. The loaf of bread had its crusts cut off and then it was iced with gooey brown molasses. Carrot curls and tiny celery slices decorated the top and the sides of the cake, which were covered with crumbled shredded wheat. What a cake! The animals would love it!

The girls made colorful party hats. The sheep had special, all-fancy ones because it was their birthday. Buttercup had a party hat made just for her, Isaac and the female goats wore hats, and so did Buzzard, the turkey. We took pictures and they ate cake and then we passed out granola bar treats and sang, "Happy birthday to you." What a party!

Keviss, the birthday boy.

"Happy birthday, Kivseh!"

Promise waiting for the cake.

THE REAL TAILS OF EASY YOKE FARM

Young Isaac in his spiffy neckerchief.

"Yummy!"

ROSEMARY RONNLUND BELCHER

Felice says, "I want to get this shot!"

"Definitely the wrong color for my complexion!" Buzzard says.

THE REAL TAILS OF EASY YOKE FARM

Precious shouts, 'Hey! My hat came off!"

Moses

One animal that hadn't appeared on the farm was my much-hoped-for llama. We looked around at farms and newspaper ads for quite a while but found nothing that I could afford. One day, as we travelled past a nearby farm, I noticed an immense, rust-colored llama. We went in to ask if he might be for sale.

I timidly knocked on the door. "I see that you have a large llama out here. Would you be interested in selling him?"

The farmer thought for a moment. "I could do that," he said cocking his head like he was thinking.

"What would you want for him?" I asked cautiously while wondering if my llama piggy bank would have enough.

He quickly named a price and as he grabbed his dirty farm coat, said, "Come out to the pasture and I'll see if I can get a hold of him so that you can have a look."

The farmer seemed to have no problem in selling the llama. He grabbed a lead and headed out into the muddy pasture. The llama ran away just to see him coming.

"I don't think that the llama likes him," Thomas commented while watching the farmer chase the huge llama around the pasture with yelling, screaming, and some nasty, unrepeatable words.

The farmer finally managed to grab the llama roughly by the halter and yanked him down so that he could attach the lead. After what seemed like a lot of wrestling, the spit-covered farmer and towering llama, drew closer. Each of them dragged and yanked the other in different directions until they made it over to where we stood.

The llama was filthy, his wool was matted, and his ear was ripped from a torn-out cattle tag. He wasn't at all friendly, but frightened and he pulled away from all touching. I felt very sorry for him.

My husband had a questioning look in his eyes. "Are you sure this is what you want?" he asked me.

I gazed into the llama's dark, suspicious eyes, and saw intelligence and beauty. I knew right then that this llama would be mine. No other llama would do!

"Yes," I answered. I would take this one.

"Oookay," Thomas agreed with obvious hesitancy.

I looked squarely at the farmer. "We'll take him."

"Alright," the farmer answered. "Let's go into the house and settle things up."

We were given a birth certificate for the llama. It had a complicated name on it. It was a long name that was difficult to say. It certainly wasn't a name that you could use when you were calling across the pasture to a llama. I took bits and pieces of his registered name and decided to name him Moses. After all, I thought, the pasture he was in was pretty much a swamp. In the Bible, Moses was pulled out of the Nile River, so in my mind it kind of fit.

The farmer told us that Moses had spent the last seven years of his life guarding a flock of sheep. Wolves, coyotes, and even dogs can attack sheep when they are out grazing. I had heard that llamas were excellent guard animals. I had just wanted a pet, but maybe Moses would like keeping an eye on our little herd for us.

Within a few days, Moses was delivered and forced kicking and spitting into a small holding and loading pen beside the barn. There, his view of his soon-to-be charges; about a dozen and a half sheep and goats, was clear and even adventurous noses could be snuffed.

I stood outside the pen watching his powerful kicks and spits. As the farmer who delivered him finally wrestled him into the pen. Moses reared up then back kicked right through a new thick board that we had just nailed up to make the pen stronger. It was two whole inches thick and ten inches wide and about ten feet long. How he had managed to do it, shocked us. We all jumped. I recalled how the llama had needed chasing down so that we could view him at his farm. Would we be able to train him or had my heart led me astray?

I talked softly to Moses, yearning to touch him but fearing to enter the pen. Moses was too frazzled and terrified to hear me. We brought water, good hay, and a goat mix of grains and molasses. He responded by sniffing everything then warily testing the hay.

Later that day, I fearfully entered the small pen, talking softly and bracing for a kick. He glanced at me and continued eating—the kick never came. The following morning, we released him into a small pasture behind the barn. I looked at his hay feeder and feed dish and noticed that the food was disappearing.

When I walked into the pasture, Moses alerted to me right away, raising his head and his long ears to listen. He stared at me with what I thought was more curiosity than fear.

I visited him every few hours, wishing he would approach to accept the treats that I offered. The only change seemed to be a subtle softening and questioning in his eyes. In fact, I thought I could detect playful curiosity, or was it my imagination?

One morning, at feeding time, I entered Moses's pasture, where the sheep and goats were grazing, and I tried to talk to him once more. He ignored me.

On a whim, I turned my back to him and slid behind a tree. I waited, ridiculing myself that this wild creature might want to play. Suddenly a huge head and long neck wrapped itself around the tree and with inches to spare, stared into my eyes. I jumped at his sudden presence. Then, laughing out loud, I ran for another tree, hiding once more. Immediately, the intelligent face was staring once more into mine.

Could I touch him? Did I dare reach out to stroke him?

No, he wanted to get to know me better first. He backed away with an amused expression on his muzzle.

Before long, we were beginning to let the sheep and goats travel from the barn pasture to a rear pasture to graze throughout the day and return at night. Moses seemed gentle, attentive enough, and happy to join the flock. He definitely seemed to be happy.

There was a problem, though. Twice a day, the flock ran past an unfenced strip of woods on a hill leading down to the creek. Although the strip was only a hundred feet long, a detour down to the creek meant a long chase for us and exposure to hungry wildlife for the flock. For Moses, it perhaps meant a long jump over the creek up the far bank, off our land and gone forever.

So, he had to take the trip on a lead. The big chase to attach a lead to his halter became a game for him. But it was an exhausting game for me because he was so tall and quick. When I was tired after a long day and dinner was threatening to burn, the struggle was even more defeating.

Moses seemed to love it. After a number of frustrating days and chases, I noticed the glimmer in his eyes and decided to call his bluff. I let the trained flock run back to the barn for dinner, and stood with the gate ajar. Blocking the entrance, with my back turned away from Moses, I raised my right arm straight into the air. I pinched the open lead clasp in my fingers and let the lead drape to the ground.

"Moses," I called, "I know you're smarter than we think! If you want to go with the others put your chin in the lead!"

Within a moment, I felt the giant body pass swiftly to my left. A pause, then he passed behind me to the right. A pause, quiet footsteps and a warm furry chin laid itself on the top of my hand only a fraction of an inch from actually hooking the loop of his halter on my lead.

I looked up, smiled, clicked the snap on the ring and shaking my head in joyful disbelief, led him to the barn. For many nights he repeated his courtesy to me until we were sure he would follow the flock.

He was the most gentle animal to lead. My arm was outstretched as high as I could reach and yet the lead reached higher. Still I felt no pressure on the lead line. It was like he wasn't there at all. Leading Moses was like guiding a helium balloon. It was an exhilarating experience of its own.

Now, Moses had joined us near his eighth birthday and his resume had declared a life of sheep herding. That winter, when my goats were treated to the luxury of the barn, the heavy-wooled sheep and their guardian were given a fenced pasture and shelter out back.

One cold snowy night, we awoke to Moses's alarm calls along with fierce barking. Llamas have a loud call that they give when something is very wrong. A human can't copy it. It sounds like a combination of a turkey gobble and a donkey bray. It is loud and unmistakable.

Thomas and I threw ourselves into some combination of clothing and raced outside. The barking was fierce—a pack of wild dogs were crawling wolf-style over the pasture fence. My husband ran ahead wielding a shovel, and I followed brandishing a flashlight.

The light revealed the truth. The fearsome, snarling pack was endeavoring to climb over a fence upon which was firmly planted a massive, woolly llama chest. Thomas and I made such a noise that the invading dogs tore away. Behind proud Moses, who was still pressed against the fence, was the horned ram, and from the shed frightened bleats and rustling were heard. All were safe.

We thanked Moses and returned to bed.

We noticed many attributes about this still-aloof fellow. In the mornings, as we let the goats out of the barn and the flocks joined together, Moses stood at the door. His head bobbed slightly as each animal passed.

"He's counting," my husband exclaimed in amazement. "He's actually counting!"

And, true to character, Moses cared for them all. We'd see him pacing frantically at the gate, desperately trying to get our attention, and sure enough, one of the flock had snuck into the neighbor's field or taken a trip down to the creek. When the criminal was returned, Moses felt free to resume his afternoon nap. If we brought the tractor into the field, every animal was firmly herded to the other end until any danger was passed.

Other llamas arrived, and every beast, including the geese, came under Moses's care. In springtime, goat kids climbed the Moses mountain, even springing off his head. All was well.

One year, my husband brought me a tiny, brown, orphaned goat kid from another farm. It was weak and underweight.

THE REAL TAILS OF EASY YOKE FARM

When Moses saw it, he impatiently paced around us and whined. Forgetting his nervousness of humans, he nuzzled close to the baby in my arms. He pushed my arm down wanting me to set the baby on the ground. As I carried the little one to the barn, what sounded like huge convulsing sobs poured out of this incredible llama.

I laid the baby kid down on some soft hay. I knew that it would have the world's best babysitter. But the little one looked up and was terrified. A mama goat, Moses was not, and so I picked the baby up and carried it into the house where we could care for him until he gained some strength.

As the llama herd increased, Moses included them in his personal herd. Even the yearling boys gave him immense respect and immediate obedience.

I recall one feisty little yearling male, who was feeling spunky one day. He was running up behind the calmly feeding mother llamas and giving them a chest bump so hard that they ended up nose first in a round bale.

This was considered very rude llama behavior. Now the moms would turn and spit at this naughty youngster, but he had quickly run off out of their range. This behavior continued for a bit and then he bumped his own mother, who wheeled around with llama fire in her angry eyes. With furious llama hums and clickings, she scolded him harshly.

He lowered his long neck below his shoulders in respect and she sent him down the end of the pasture to Moses. That little llama cringed all the way across the field and stood before the massive guardian llama with neck lowered and tail raised over his back in submission. Moses said a few angry things to the rude young male with loud clicking noises. Then he sent him off to the corner of the pasture by himself. He didn't allow the lonely and sorry little fellow back with the herd until he felt that the young one had been well punished.

One afternoon, a friend of ours drove his pickup into the pasture to get some manure for his garden. The flock was way down the other end of the field, except for two venturesome crias. Cria is the name that baby llamas are called. This friendly farmer had a pocket full of crunchies for just such an occasion. The little ones were just licking their lips when an angry brown whirlwind, with ears pinned back and tongue clicking, raced across the field.

Two crias were firmly sent to the barn until further notice and Moses, the large sentry, went out and paced back and forth in front of the truck's grill until the farmer had filled his truck. Then Moses escorted the amazed farmer out of the pasture gate and watched him drive out the driveway.

At Christmas time, we put a life-size, very realistic manger scene in the pasture. The tall, loyal fellow watched us setting it up year after year. He dutifully made his rounds, sniffing each large figure and animal in the scene. Then he guarded the Holy Family by day and night. The flock joined him under the warm spotlights, making the manger scene as living as it could be. Newspapers took pictures, crowds gathered for weeks, and a little boy was heard to remark,

"Momma, the Wise Men have come. The camels are there!" Now we certainly didn't have real camels on the farm, much to my sorrow, but giant Moses certainly looked convincing as he hovered closely on a winter's evening.

Spring came in all its beauty and when the pasture next to us was blooming with fragrant alfalfa, one of our female llamas, Taya, decided that she would jump the fence and enjoy a romp. She paused briefly, I hope because she had a conscience, then nimbly leapt over the fence. Noticing the frolicking llama's escape, her friends, Jaycee, Kaloka, Juanita, Penny, and the other momma llamas, along with their very willing youngsters of various ages sailed over the fence with ease. They began cavorting in the neighbour's field.

"Oh no," I cried, "the llamas are out!"

Thomas, Rob, Paul, David, Jeremy, Crystal, and Melody all came running at my cry. We all grabbed wands from the barn and headed out the pasture gate. A wand is a long piece of thin plastic. It is not used to hit the llama but as an extension of the human's arms.

So here we were, out hip-deep in alfalfa, with our arms outstretched trying to get the herd rounded up together and back into the barnyard.

One llama hadn't jumped out. After all he was the herd disciplinarian and he had scruples. Moses stood on a little hill right beside the fence and watched and watched. We just got the herd back to the fence-line when Taya kicked up her heels with a playful and defiant twirl. She leapt back out into the field, drawing all of the other llamas behind her.

Over and over we got them rounded up but then away they leapt. We were exhausted. We tried luring them with grain and crunchies—we tried everything we could think of. Finally, tired of watching our puny efforts, the mighty guardian of the pastures took a huge leap directly from the little hill and out into the field. I saw him jump and my first sentence was, "Oh no, not you too!"

But we didn't have to worry. Moses flew at top speed across the field right to up the sneaky Taya. He leaped around her and quickly began herding. She followed him. All the other wayward llamas quickly formed a group with Moses at the head and he led them right through the pasture gate into the barnyard. What a guy!

Moses also pulled a little cart for us sometimes. A ride down the side of the highway was exciting indeed. The scary part was on the way back when he saw the windmill and knew that home and barn were near. There was no holding him back and you got the ride of your life. He pulled kids around on picnics, and he even took my elderly mom for a wonderful ride.

Later that year, we had a very sad moment. One of our llama mommas had a cria that died at birth. Although we tried to help, the baby just wouldn't start breathing but lay limp on the grass. I knew that if I took the dead cria away that the mom would frantically search for it. I had to leave it until she was ready to leave it herself.

A strange and beautiful thing happened. At first, we heard heartbreaking llama sobs that sounded just like human crying. This momma was mourning her lost little one. Moses herded all of the curious llama onlookers away from her and didn't allow them near the sorrowful momma all morning.

In the afternoon, he stood in front of the herd and allowed the llamas one by one to go up to the grieving mom and respectfully sniff the baby, offering their condolences. Then they walked away to allow the next llama to pay their little visit. It took most of an hour, this little llama funeral, and then the momma slowly stood up and walked away from her dead cria. She headed for the back pasture under the trees and lay down. I went over to the lifeless little one, picked it up gently, and took it away.

The sorrowing momma remained in the back pasture. She wouldn't come for meals, she wouldn't move. I went out often and talked gently to her, but as a mom, I personally understood the pain of losing a child. So, I allowed her to grieve.

Four days later, I knew that I had to get this momma to eat something. I went out and picked some delicious wildflowers; a big and pretty bouquet. I walked up to the momma, talking softly. Kneeling down, I offered her the lovely flowers. She sniffed and then reached out her long neck and began to nibble. Llamas don't use vases, that long neck serves them quite nicely. As I visited, she downed the offering, and then stood up.

She raised her head up high, and pointed her nose at a branch of fresh leaves on the overhead tree. They were out of her reach, but I knew that she was asking me if I'd get them for her.

I grabbed a shepherd's crook and reached up to the lovely green clump of leaves. I pulled it downward and strained to break it off. Finally, I had it: about four foot of leaves and two feet of strong branch. I handed the branch to the waiting momma, leaves first. She took it but then dropped it on the ground. I was curious, and as I watched she picked up the branch end close to where the leaves began. She headed over to the chain-link fence and firmly rammed it into the fence at about four-foot height. Now the leaves were hanging out from the fence at a comfortable eating height and she went to work having a good meal.

After that the momma walked out into the front pasture and rejoined the herd. Moses got up from lying in the sun and came to sniff her nose and welcome her back.

The story of Moses could just continue on and on. He became the most faithful pasture guard that we could ever have. His intelligence was overwhelming. His loyalty and sense of duty were immeasurable. Did he ever allow us to hand feed him? Oh yes, those huge jaws soon learned that treats were very acceptable. Horse crunchies, granola bars, and carrots. That big fellow would take a complete, foot-long, farm-grown carrot in his mouth from back to front and you could never tell that anything was there until the crunching began. He was a champ and an inspiration. To think that I could have left him out in that original farm pasture, dirty, hungry, and unappreciated.

Moses proves that the outside of an individual doesn't always show their true worth. How fortunate we all are that our Lord and Savior reassures us.

THE REAL TAILS OF EASY YOKE FARM

For man looketh on the outward appearance, but the LORD looketh on the heart. 1 Samuel 16:7

Moses stands guard.

Everything Grows Well on a Farm!

The vegetables in the garden grew to the biggest we'd ever seen. The strawberries and raspberries grew sweet and beautiful. The flowers filled the gardens with fragrant beauty and the farm grew with new pastures and shelters, and fences and…our wonderful llamas Kaloka, Juanita, Jaycee, Cecilia, Penny, Taya, and their families, and of course Moses.

These new ladies had been chosen to become our llama mommas. Some of them had long, soft wool. Each year we would shear their wool and either sell it to crafters or send it away to be made into lovely garments or even nice socks. Their crias would also be wool llamas. Kaloka, Jaycee, and Penny were taller and had shorter wool. Their crias would be raised to be pasture guardians, pack llamas for hikers, or even quick-cart llamas. Three amazing daddy studs; Teddy, Blazer, and Legacy also came to live at our farm. They were all handsome and had won lots of llama-show ribbons and trophies. Before long the farm grew with many new crias being born. Some of their names were Pokey, Treasure, and CJ.

Before many years had passed, we had more than thirty beautiful registered llamas living on the farm. We trained them and shampooed and brushed them very nicely. A number of them went with us to llama shows where they won trophies and ribbons.

We didn't grow just in our llama herd, A red horse named Spitfire arrived to keep Prince company. The goats continued growing their families and so did Buttercup and Blossom, who gave birth to a calf, who was dark-brown on both ends with a thick, white, even stripe down the middle. The cute little calf looked just like an Oreo cookie, so we named her Cookie. Now it was true that we had a dog whose name was Cookie before we moved up north, but if you saw this little calf you would know that no other name would suit her. What a lot of growing! I didn't even mention the sheep, the barn-cat families, the colorful chickens, and our flock of turkeys.

People began asking if they could come and visit. Schools brought classes of excited school children. I showed the children how to card and spin the llama wool. I taught them about the countries where llamas come from and the different kinds of llamas; llamas, alpacas, guanacos and vicunas. The small vicunas were so soft and special that in the old days only the kings and queens were allowed to wear clothing made from their wool.

As the children watched the llamas play with their llama toys, we offered them cookies and juice. Then we gave them baggies of llama treats and set them free to run in the pastures feeding and petting the animals. At the end of the afternoon, their teachers would take the happy, tired children back to school carrying special bags with coloring pages, the wool that they had hand-spun, instant pictures of them with the llamas, balloons with llamas pictures on them, and other small souvenirs that reminded them of what they had learned.

I loved it when the schools came! I loved seeing the eyes of the children light up as they learned new things and laughed at my playful llamas. I loved watching the timid and shy children relax when the soft head and neck of a llama came to cuddle up to them. And I loved seeing the teachers relax and enjoy themselves. I guess that I just loved doing special things for people.

The Lord had given us this beautiful farm, and we'd given it back to him for his use. After one wonderful day of hosting school children, I had an idea. Maybe there was another way to help people enjoy the farm. Maybe we could import special llama and alpaca items from Peru and Ecuador and have our own farm store. I was sure that lots of people would love to see things that they had never seen before and would maybe take some of them home with them.

We had a historic log building out by the pasture. We had used it as a guest house and a haven for lost travelers and tourists whose vehicles just happened to break down right on the highway right in front of our farm. They had travelled a long way and were often heading to Alaska. The families that sat at the side of the road were often tired and forlorn. Sometimes they were in tears. We towed them into the driveway, welcomed them into the little log guest house, fed them, and often had a lovely and memorable visit with them over the next days as their vehicle was being repaired in town. They relaxed, the smiles returned, and the animals comforted and cheered them. Eventually we waved goodbye to new and lasting friends.

The little log house could make a wonderful little store. Stranded folks could always be welcomed into our home. Our kids were all grown up and gone by this time. We had lots of room inside.

I said, "Thomas, what would you think of opening a farm store in the log house?" I went on to describe my new dream to his listening ears.

"I guess that would be okay," he replied thoughtfully. "Do you think that you could make it work?"

"I'm sure I could," I answered.

"You understand that you'd end up having to do all the bookwork that goes with it?" he questioned me, while looking at me with raised eyebrows knowing that I really didn't like bookkeeping at all.

I thought about the extra bookkeeping for a moment and decided that It couldn't get much worse than it was now.

"And what about importing the items that you want from other countries? You haven't got a clue about how to go about that."

"I can learn," I replied confidently. "Other people do it, why can't I?"

"Well," Thomas replied with a bit of a shoulder shrug, "if you figure that you can make a go of it and run a business, not just a hobby, then it's fine with me."

Within the next few weeks the renovations took place, as we scoured ads for counters, clothing racks, and glass-front jewelry and display cases.

I ordered a sign that said, "Easy Yoke Farm Store." And I found a huge wooden ox yoke that we hung over the door. A yoke over the shoulders helps a person or animal to carry a bigger load more comfortably. In some countries people still use yokes to help them carry things.

We had named our farm Easy Yoke Farm from a scripture verse where Jesus says: *"Come unto me, all ye that labour and are heavy laden, and I will give you rest. Take my yoke upon you, and learn of me; for I am meek and lowly in heart: and ye shall find rest unto your souls. For my yoke is easy, and my burden is light."* Matthew 11: 28-30

We wanted our farm to be a place of rest for both animals and humans.

Soon it was time to place my first order for all the new items that I wanted to sell. I found importers who were more than willing to work with me. I found jewelers who made beautiful llama jewelry, and a potter in Alberta who created amazing vases and bowls using outline paintings of actual animals from our farm. I found veterinary companies for basic medical supplies and companies to supply animal halters and hardware. I wanted it to be a one-stop shop for many farmer's needs.

The big boxes began arriving. Many were packed in newspapers in a language that I couldn't read. It was like Christmas, but unloading all the boxes and recording all of my purchases took more than one morning.

Finally, the store was ready to open.

A cozy little woodstove gently warmed the welcoming interior. The newly cleaned and varnished logs and wooden floor glowed in the lamplight. Crystal's dried bouquets of wildflowers hung in baskets from the rafters, and the windows were charmed by farmy, checkered, red tieback curtains.

Just inside the door, a counter displayed containers of smaller items like llama pens, pencils with llama heads on them, a bowl of children's llama rings, and original llama postcards as well as photo postcards of the llamas and other animals on our farm. There were even llama lollipops and chocolate llamas.

In the case beneath, beautiful silver belt buckles and bracelets, rested on soft velvet, beside the exquisite llama pottery in warm earthy colors.

On nearby shelves groups of very fluffy soft teddy bears made of Alpaca wool in all their natural colors sat patiently waiting for little visitors. I had ordered teddies in sizes from tiny to an armful so that every child could take one home. Beside them stood rows of fluffy standing llamas and alpacas with colorful native halters. There were wee little llamas, middle-sized llamas, and one giant llama, who was the size of a real llama cria, guarded them from the floor. Farm-made toy llamas in felt and fun fur stood alongside and went out the door in the arms of many happy children. Solid maple llama figures that were painted to look just like our llamas along with story books, coloring books, and crayons filled a kid's section.

Real Peruvian instruments that you could learn to play filled another section of the store. Some had strings, some were like drums, some were like little flutes. I was sure that the children would especially love the little clay bird ocarinas that looked and sounded just like the birds in the trees. I loved the wooden Pan flutes that came in all sizes and prices. I had also ordered wonderful Peruvian music and it softly played in the store and danced across the pastures, whenever the store was open.

Thomas had made me a special wooden rack that looked like a full-size standing llama. Across its back lay ornately patterned alpaca blankets, which also filled a shelf in a tall wooden wardrobe also created by my husband. Soft llama and alpaca jackets for men, ladies, and children were carefully hung on hangers. Scarves, gloves, hats, and toques with pictures of llamas knitted on them sat neatly stacked on shelves. We sold exquisite fine wool sweaters for both ladies and men, adorable sweaters for the kids, and both adult purses and cute little children's purses.

A glass jewelry case displayed intricate silver and gold jewelry, as well as unique and delicate earrings.

On the other side of the store, we sold llama and goat halters, collars, leads, and wands as well as some basic veterinary supplies and special bottles for feeding animal babies. There was so much in that little amazing little store.

THE REAL TAILS OF EASY YOKE FARM

People could shop for hours and then take their purchases home in our specially designed llama bags.

I looked at the charming country store and knew that It was time to open up the farm. Easy Yoke Farm pamphlets were distributed to tourist information centers in both BC and Alberta, offering daily farm visits, farm tour Saturdays, and special openings for tour buses and school classes. The store would be open every day but Sunday.

I might have mentioned that everything grows on a farm. Our Farm became very popular and we entertained visitors from all over the world. The pastures often sounded like a meeting at the United Nations. The animals grew, our responsibilities grew, and our ability to make others happy also grew.

In the end, the farm grew in more ways than we ever could have imagined. Everything grew well on our farm!

Dear little farm store in the winter.

The Gift of Treasure

One of our lovely llama ladies had a secret. She was getting ready to criate. That meant that she was going to give birth to a baby llama.

Day after day we waited for the happy birth to take place. One afternoon it happened, and a beautiful cria was born. She was a big baby with silky, dark, orangy-red wool. I could see that she was going to be a very special llama. We named her Treasure.

All babies, even little human babies, need to drink milk from their mommies soon after they are born. This helps them to grow strong. Little crias must stand on their long legs so that they can nurse from their mommies and drink the special milk.

I watched little Treasure trying to stand up on her long spindly new legs. Something wasn't right. Little Treasure tried to stand, but her legs wouldn't hold her up and she fell down again. Over and over she tried and fell down on the grass. I watched carefully and saw a problem. Her long front legs had been squeezed tight inside her mommy while she was growing and were bent backward at what we would call her wrist. She had no strength to straighten them out. She just couldn't stand up. What could we do?

I went for my little animal-doctor kit and got out some bright-pink, elastic vet wrap. I carefully padded the little front legs with cotton batting to keep them straight and then wrapped them snuggly with the bright pink wrap. When I set her back on her legs, she found that she could stand up, and with a little help was able to nurse just fine. Now I had a new cria with bright pink socks.

Every day, I gave Treasure a little treat, loosened the bright pink socks, massaged the little legs, and re-wrapped them. It took about six long weeks before Treasure's little legs had become straight and gained the strength to let her run and jump and play.

Treasure had become very friendly. She loved to have hugs. She loved to be cuddled. She thought that was what I was doing when I held her over my lap and re-wrapped her little legs. Treasure simply loved and trusted people.

As Treasure grew into beautiful llama, with long, dark, orangy-red wool, she became a favorite to the many visitors that came to the farm.

You already know that we had a little store on the farm that sold lovely wool sweaters, jackets, teddy bears, and other wonderful items that I brought from Peru and Ecuador. Many people came to the store, and Treasure was right there near the fence to welcome them.

The farm also became a place where some people would just come to talk to us. Sometimes they were just sad, or maybe something difficult had happened in their lives.

Surprisingly, even with the hustle and bustle that went on at the farm they told us that it was such a place of peace.

One day, I heard the very loud roar of a motorcycle coming down the long farm driveway. I stepped outside the store and watched a big, burly biker climb off a huge motorcycle that I think that they call a hog.

He was dressed in black leathers and tall boots that had many laces up the side of them. He took off his jacket and I could see his torn-off sleeves and muscular arms covered in tattoos right down to his knuckles. On his head was a German-style helmet, and out from the bottom of the helmet poured a huge clump of curly, dark, orangy-red hair.

I have to admit that I didn't like the look of this fellow, especially because I was alone on the farm that day and he looked kind of snarly and scary.

I went over to him and politely asked, "Can I help you, sir?"

I *was* hoping that he would answer, "Can you tell me where the nearest gas station is?" and be on his way.

Instead he gruffly mumbled, "I'm here to see the llamas."

At that point, I didn't think that I wanted him out with my "babies," but what could I do? This was a farm that offered farm tours.

I led him over to the wide pasture gate and slowly pulled back the long board that held the two fence sections together. I held it open, and the heavy, burly biker entered the pasture.

Now, friendly Treasure was out grazing and lifted up her head to see who was coming. She couldn't believe her eyes.

Not only were we going to have a visitor, but he had the most beautiful hair that she had ever seen on a human. She started over in full gallop. The big burly biker saw her running full speed. His eyes widened, and he stepped back grabbing the gate in fear. "Does it bite?" he stammered breathlessly.

"No!" I reassured him. "She just wants a ..." Well there was no time for explanations because Treasure had arrived and her long, dark, orangy-red neck hung over the biker's tensed shoulders with her nose buried in that clump of curly, dark, orangy-red hair.

I added the word "hug" to complete my previous sentence.

Treasure cuddled close and stood still. Slowly, the muscular burly arms reached out and wrapped gently around Treasure's neck. Treasure cuddled closer. Then the big burly arms hugged her firmly, rocking a little back and forth, and a smile began to creep across the big burly biker's face. He not only smiled, he grinned big and his cold blue eyes began to twinkle with joy.

"What's itsh' name?" he asked while smiling and hugging. He did seem to have a little difficulty pronouncing his words. Maybe that's why he didn't say much.

"Her name is Treasure," I answered, marvelling at the change that a little love could bring.

"Treashure." He repeated her name with such softness and gentleness that I couldn't believe that it was the same man.

We did the pasture tour, but I doubt that he saw very much. His tender eyes were on his new friend, who walked closely by his side. His arm never left that long, dark, orangy-red neck.

At the end of the tour, the biker paused at the gate and spent more time gently hugging Treasure and saying lots of soft words that only she could hear. As he left, he looked back, smiling and shaking his head sadly. He stared at Treasure once more and said tenderly, "Shweetheart, if I had a sidecar, I'd take you with me." Then, he put on his black leather jacket and roared his noisy hog down the farm driveway. Treasure watched her new friend drive away.

That night there were thunder showers and the dust bowls that the llamas loved to roll in turned to yucky mud. Treasure wasn't bothered, she was going to take her morning bath anyway and rolled with enthusiasm.

When I saw her, I couldn't believe the dirt and mud that dripped off her previously lovely, dark, orangy-red wool. *Oh well,* I thought, *when the sun comes out, she will dry and all the dirt will just fall out.*

I was surprised when I saw a very expensive car driving carefully down towards me and I thought it must just be a customer for the store.

An elderly woman stepped out of the car. She looked amazing. Her silvery hair was perfect. She had lovely earrings that fell onto a thick, silver-fox fur collar. Beneath the collar was a beautiful, violet ,velvet coat with thick, silver-fox fur cuffs. She wore lovely, grey leather gloves and had a perfect leather bag to match. She was just plain beautiful. I looked forward to showing her the many pretty things in the store.

She had other things in mind.

"I'd like to go in and see the llamas," she asked politely.

"Ma'am, I answered, "it rained last night and those llamas have been rolling and are very dirty. I'd be very afraid of you getting your lovely coat ruined."

"Please take me in and let me see the llamas," she said politely but with determination. She headed to the farm gate and began unlatching the gate herself.

"I'm so worried about your clothing," I pleaded as I noticed a friendly, dark orangy-red llama covered in drippy mud, trotting happily towards the lady and gaining speed as she came.

Soon Treasure was at a full gallop. "I yelled "No!" to the excited llama, but it was too late. Treasure had spied that lovely silver-fox collar, and thrown her muddy self into the woman's outstretched arms.

I gasped and cringed as I watched the beautiful, violet, velvet coat becoming covered in little trickles of gooey, drippy, dirty pasture mud. *Oh, the dry-cleaning bills!* I thought with horror.

I grabbed Treasure and tried to pull her away.

"No, please," the woman begged. She tightly hugged Treasure while hiding her own head in the dirty neck. Then I heard them—sobs, becoming louder, but not for the ruined coat. They were from a deeply broken heart that only a patient, loving llama could soothe.

I watched the woman rock Treasure, crying loudly, then sobbing softly. I felt embarrassed at watching this very personal and private meeting. After many minutes, the elderly woman backed away from Treasure. In a very polite voice she said, "Thank you." Then she headed out the gate, and drove way.

I stood in peaceful wonder as I watched her leave. My heart was deeply touched. Our Treasure went back to grazing with the other llamas, ready to share her gift with whoever needed her.

*Many waters cannot quench love,
neither can the floods drown it:* Sol 8:7

A young Treasure.

CJ Learns Contentment.

"He's out again!" my husband called in a frustrated voice from an upstairs bedroom. He could see a young white llama frisking around the yard where he shouldn't be. I looked out and sure enough, CJ was out of his pen again.

CJ was a handsome llama, who was soon to celebrate his second birthday. He was white all over except for the brown patches on his cheeks and a brown, heart-shaped marking around his nose. He also had a fluffy grey tail.

CJ shared a pasture with three friends; Avi, Joshua, and Buddy and they spent their days wrestling and leaping and rolling around in their dust bowl. They had lots of nice green grass to eat, hay to enjoy, fresh water, and good grain. CJ should have been a very contented young llama, but he wasn't content. He spent his time looking outside of his pasture at the other grass and plants that lined the driveway and grew in the other pastures.

Instead of eating and playing with the other "boys" he began stretching his long neck under the fence to see if he could taste something just beyond his reach. Before long, he found that the wire fence was changing shape and there was more of him outside of the fence than inside.

CJ wiggled a little bit more and there he was, lying outside of the fence. He stood up happily and began nibbling all of the nice things that he had been longing for. As he munched on pretty flowers and lovely leaves, he wondered why his friends didn't squeeze under the fence and join him.

What CJ didn't understand was that his fence had protected him from all kinds of danger. The highway was close by with cars and trucks racing down it. There were other farm animals bigger than he was who would love to hurt him if he got into their pasture uninvited. Amongst the beautiful, colorful, even tasty flowers and shrubs were plants that were poisonous and could make him very sick, blind, or even dead.

CJ was too busy enjoying his freedom to realize what danger he was in.

That's when my husband noticed that he was out and the two of us chased the quick llama with long legs, who didn't want to be caught. We caught him, haltered him, and put him back with his friends.

Was he happy? He was content for a few hours, but then he began longing for the green grass outside of his pasture again. Soon, he found another way out and was caught and put back in. The next time he simply jumped over the fence and found that he could jump it easily. This time he wasn't put back in with his friends. He was put into a little pen that he could not escape from.

CJ was so sad and lonely. He watched his friends playing in the larger pasture where the grass looked so fresh and good. He longed to roll in the old dust bowl and rest in the shade of the big tree.

After a few days, CJ was put back with his friends once more. This time he didn't look for ways to get out. He didn't covet the green grass and pretty flowers. He was contented to be back with his friends and realized that he had everything that he really needed all along.

Be content with such things as ye have: Hebrews 13:5

CJ.

Precious

I told you the story about how little Precious was born. She was not white like the other goats on the farm. She was not even white like her mommy, Rachel. She was black with little white stripes down the sides of her nose. She was so sweet that we named her Precious.

Precious as a newborn.

THE REAL TAILS OF EASY YOKE FARM

Precious was an Alpine goat. Alpine goats came from the high mountains. They love to climb and jump and run in places where other goats or people would certainly slip and fall. When Precious was still a tiny kid goat, she began running and jumping every chance she got. She jumped on hay bales. She jumped on other goats. She jumped on the backs of sleeping cows. She ran right down the back of a big horse that was trying to sleep. She ran from his tail all the way to his nose and when he raised it up to say, "Hey!" she sprang right off the end of his nose and landed on the top of the big round bale. Precious loved to jump and climb.

One afternoon, when the other little goat kids were napping, Precious went exploring and climbed way up in the barn rafters where the smaller hay bales were stored. We heard her bleating and crying for help. She was just a baby after all. She had gotten up by herself but just didn't have the courage to get down the same way.

"Precious is stuck up in the barn," Melody called to me. "And I can't get her down. She won't come to me."

I went out and looked up to see a small goat, stepping back and forth and looking downward, but afraid to jump.

"Come on, baby," I called and tried to encourage her to jump down again. I guess she thought, *Okay, Mom's here* and she jumped, but not the same way that she'd climbed up. Suddenly, I felt four little hooves land right on my shoulder and the sure-footed little Alpine goat stood happily beside my head where she had landed.

Precious lived with her family in a cute little goat house in the back pasture. The girls and I had painted shutters with vines and flowers and it was as sweet as could be. Precious soon found that she could easily jump onto the roof of the goat house. She would gallop on that roof, and run right to the very edge where she looked like she was going to fall off. Then she would take a big leap, twirling in the air, and she landed safely back on the roof to run and jump some more.

People who visited our farm began calling Precious the Dancing Goat. They would stand for hours and oooh and ahhh as she leapt and danced and twirled on the little goat house roof. Almost every day people would be coming to the door with cameras and grandchildren and friends, waiting on the doorstep.

"Could we go out and watch your dancing goat?" they asked with grins of anticipation.

"Of course," I told them and off they went to stand by the fence and oooh and awwww.

The local newspaper even printed a story about her with a picture of her with her hooves right off the ground, twirling in the air.

One day, I found her outside the barnyard fence and wandering around the yard. That worried me because the highway was nearby and that was no place for a little goat to be playing. I put her back in the barnyard only to find that she soon escaped again.

We had guests visiting the farm and they and their children were eating breakfast at a long picnic table. They were having a wonderful farm vacation. From the table they could look over the fence and watch all the fun things that were happening in the barnyard.

Suddenly, breakfast came to a stop. There in the middle of the picnic table, beside the jug of unspilled milk, the boxes of cereal, and the plates of yummy food, stood a happy-looking little Alpine goat. She had landed without spilling a drop. The children laughed and squealed with delight. Even the parents laughed at this uninvited surprise guest at their breakfast table. I heard the noise and loud laughter from the house. Looking out I saw Precious, accepting pats and cheers from a table full of surprised guests. The cameras had appeared. This would be a breakfast that none of our guests would ever forget.

How did she get there? I wondered. I could see that she had jumped right off the roof of the chicken shed and on to the table, but how did she get onto the chicken shed roof?

I put a little rope on Precious and led her back to the barnyard where the rest of her family stood watching. They knew the secret, but weren't telling.

For days I watched, trying to figure out the little goat's secret. One day, I saw an amazing sight. Remember the horse that had put up with the little goat running down his back? Well, maybe he liked the back rub, because here he was helping Precious to escape.

Spitfire was lying down minding his own business. Precious jumped on his back and quietly asked for a favor. Spitfire agreed and stood up with his surefooted passenger now riding wherever they were going. Spitfire headed for the side of the red barn. He stood still while Precious took a leap and began climbing the big barn roof. She knew exactly where she was going. She climbed right over to the other side where she took an easy little leap onto the roof of the chicken shed. Over the chicken shed roof she pranced, stopping at the edge on the other side. There she joyfully jumped onto the grass in the yard below.

I could hardly believe my eyes, and who do you scold, the smart little Alpine goat, or the big horse?

We were going to have to think about how to stop Precious from escaping.

It was about that time that we began to notice that something was growing on the top of Precious's little head; two little horns. She was pretty gentle so we didn't really worry about her butting anybody and hurting them. Those little horns grew and we just got used to them.

There was another mystery in the barnyard that was making us wonder. As you know, we had a little herd of lovely llamas on the farm. We had mommas and babies and even three handsome daddies. We kept their dinner in a big old freezer in the barn. The freezer wasn't plugged in, but inside there were three different spaces for grain.

The first space was for sweet dried molasses, which all of the animals loved sprinkled on top of their dinner or mixed into their grain. The next space was for grain that was already mixed; oats, barley, corn in the winter time, molasses, and a bit of salt. The last space had a bag of barley, a bag of oats, a bag of corn, and sometimes a bag of wheat and a smaller bag of salt. The llamas and goats were pretty excited at mealtimes and would line up and jostle each other outside the barn door waiting impatiently for us to fill the buckets to fill everyone's dinner dishes, which were hooked onto the white, three-board fence.

Early one morning, at feeding time, Tom and I went out to the barn and the llamas and goats were already crowding into the barn and seemed to be munching excitedly. Inside, the grain freezer was wide open. The long-necked llamas were pushing and shoving each other to get their noses into the freezer. Some of the bigger goats were standing on their hind legs and also trying to reach in.

How had this happened? We called our kids and said loudly, "Who left the grain freezer open?"

"I didn't. Not me. Uh uh, I wasn't even out at the barn," came the many replies. Everyone said that it sure wasn't them.

We couldn't believe that, so we closed up the freezer lid, and finished the morning chores. It was not healthy for the animals to eat extra grain, and they wouldn't be happy if the freezer ended up empty before we were able to fill it again.

The next day, guess what? The llamas and goats served themselves breakfast again! Once again, we called out our kids and told them that there was no way that this could happen on its own.

We checked the latch on the freezer lid and everything seemed to be working fine. Our grain stores were going down. We weren't pleased.

That evening as I headed out for chores, I noticed a commotion around the barn doors. This time I could see the freezer just fine. There stood a little Alpine goat—Precious! She was half-standing on her hind legs and had one horn hooked under the latch of the freezer lid. She was working to lift it with the skill of a safecracker. Taya, who was a tall llama, stood patiently watching the smart little black and white at work. Suddenly the latch lifted and the lid raised just a bit. Taya shoved first her nose and then her long neck under the lid and the freezer was open to the crowd that waited outside. I think they all cheered!

From that evening onward, extra buckets, boxes, and bags: anything heavy were left on top of the grain freezer lid. Early breakfast in the barn got stopped. And at the side of the barn we strung a piece of orange snow fence so that our little Alpine couldn't go out for breakfast either. Precious may have been trying to help her friends, but in the end helping them sneak extra grain, was not a good idea.

That ye may walk honestly toward them that are without, and that ye may have lack of nothing. 1Th 4:12

Flea

The phone rang: "I've got a little goat here, born this morning," a woman's voice informed me without so much as a hello. "She's healthy, but less than four pounds. Her mother died, and I haven't got time to bottle feed her. Would you take her?"

"Umm. I guess so," I answered, knowing that I always had my girls who were willing to take on bottle feeding a little one if I couldn't find time.

"I'll bring her over," the woman replied quickly as if she was in a hurry and she hung up the phone.

I shook my head and thought, *You would think that we had a big sign up on the road:*

Bring us your sick and unwanted animals and we'll take them in and care for them.

People brought us cats and kittens, and sheep and goats, and even birds healthy or sick, and in they came and soon they were running around healthy and happy. We gave them loving care and often some needed herbs and even the vet was impressed and called us for little tidbits of advice on her ailing patients.

Within the hour, a little red car drove down the driveway and a woman in a denim dress with straight, grey hair quickly stepped out cradling a small bundle no larger than a kitten. "I named her Flea," she said as she handed the little one over. "Hope that she does well," she said abruptly and she wheeled around, climbed into her car, and drove away.

The tiny white goat was so frail and bony. I held her in one hand as I rummaged around in a drawer to find a bottle and hunted further to find a nipple that I thought she might accept. I was on the farm alone that day, but we had ample milk around so I warmed some up, filled the bottle, and holding the little one firmly on my lap, tried to persuade her to let me put the nipple into her mouth. It was a struggle, but soon she was drinking like she was starving and her little tail was wagging like a happy pup.

Of course, with winter coming on, Flea would have to be in the house, so the next hurdle was finding some newborn baby Huggies that would fit. They had to be put on upside down with the tapes on the top. Then a baby onesie would have to be put on, also upside down to hold the diaper in place. I found both, and Flea was quite co operative and looked adorable by the time I was through.

Now just like when a baby drinks, little goats drool and drip and their clothes get damp. The next chore, with Flea in one arm along for the ride, was to find an appropriate bib. It had to be one with a stretchy neck that would fit over the goat's little head and stay put while I fed her. A bib with ties wouldn't work because I already knew from experience that little goats love few things more than undoing the ties on bibs or anything else that they can sabotage.

I found a bib and set her down on the floor, while I began fixing supper. Our dogs Punkin, now a grown momma, and her pup, Biscuit, came to investigate the new little footsteps and found themselves nose to nose with Flea. They sniffed and snuffled, and Flea bounced around a little bit on her weak new legs and then followed them into the living room.

"You guys are babysitting!" I called after the dogs.

I know it sounds crazy, but these dogs had been pretty good babysitters before for all of the little stray animals that had started out in the farmhouse and not in the farmyard.

At dinner, Thomas and Melody arrived home and met Flea. Crystal was away at school, and the boys were working and had found their own apartments.

"Hello, little one," crooned Melody, cuddling Flea closely and stroking the bony little body. She fixed a bottle after milking and fed the hungry new goat. Bottle feeding would be an every two-to-three-hour task for the next month or so.

Where would Flea sleep? I knew that I would have to be feeding her a few times during the night and also be up changing diapers. I decided to put a little box down beside our bed where I could reach down and pet the little one if she was restless and easily feed her, even just by reaching over the side of the bed, if need be.

At bedtime, I folded up a small baby blanket onto the bottom of the small box and even found a cute doll blanket in the girl's room to cover Flea with. She was fed her bedtime bottle cozied up in the box and she easily went off to little-goat dream land.

Flea at 2 AM decides that her little bed is just too small.

Flea was quite a good little goat and she ate well. By the end of two weeks when I stood her up by the sink to give her a little wash and change her diaper and onesie, she reached down, picked up the folded diaper off the pile, and handed it to me at the right time. At night she happily lay down in her little bed box. Then she reached over and pulled the blanket over herself to go to sleep. When the little box began to look cramped for her, I was startled to find her missing in the middle of one night. I got up quickly and found the goat in her bright pink onesie stretched out halfway up the carpeted stairs. One little leg was dangling over the step, and she was sound asleep.

Flea was constantly following the dogs everywhere and life with a tiny goat in the house was generally pretty good.

When the spring came and some of the snow began to melt and expose the green grass in the yard. she was still pretty tiny. A small fenced area, near the back door, already had grass and the sun was shining warmly on it. I decided to let Flea out to romp a bit and put my two four-legged babysitters in with her to keep an eye out and keep her company.

As I worked around the house, I heard barking and looked out to see two dogs and a goat up on top of the wood pile piled against the garage. They were barking and bleating, and all three were wagging their tails excitedly as they searched for some squirrels hiding in the stacked wood.

That little goat thinks she is a dog, I thought to myself. That thought became even stronger when I heard barking coming from the highway and found that two naughty dogs and a little goat in a onesie were on the highway chasing cars. That would not do!

At the end of the driveway just beside the road stood a group of rural mailboxes. The post lady would deliver the mail to each farm's little box and then head on to the next set. Our dogs had begun running down the driveway and stood barking raucously and wagging their tails whenever she came to fill the boxes. She was a dog lover and knew that they weren't vicious, so she came up to the house to ask us why they were standing there barking at her. She knew that they were trying to tell her something.

"I know that they're not barking at me," she said with a thoughtful look. "I wonder what they want?"

"Do you have any extra junk mail?" I asked. That's like asking a dog if it has any extra fleas.

"Yes," she answered with a quizzical look. "Why?"

"Give the dogs each a little junk mail and see what happens," I replied.

The next day, when the dogs came to greet and bark at her, she handed each dog a mouthful of mail and watched them head joyously to the farmhouse. Now she knew.

This year, there was another little problem. Our dogs had fleas—well, our dogs had a Flea, who was just as excited to see the mail lady and just as interested in being awarded a mouth full of mail.

I worried a little about Flea. I wondered if she would ever think that she was a goat. She was also growing little horns, so no one was going to push her around.

One afternoon, I had put Flea out one more time with her sitters so that I could tidy up the house. It had snowed again, but the ground near the house was pretty dry, so out went, Punkin, Biscuit, and Flea.

They all seemed quite content to lounge on the brick patio in the sunlight and so I went into the house.

Then the phone rang and it turned into a much longer conversation than I had expected. When I hung up, I put the receiver down and suddenly remembered that I had a little goat in a onesie running around with two not totally responsible dog babysitters. I quickly peered out into the yard where I had left them. They weren't there!

I hurried outside and called. "Punkin, Biscuit, Flea! Come on, guys!" I clapped my hands together and yelled as loudly as I could. "Puuuunkin, Biiiiscuit, Fleeeea!"

No answer.

They were nowhere in sight. *Oh no*, I worried. Were they out on the highway chasing cars again?

Then, I heard barking. Far away barking. It was coming from way down the creek, away down past our property line, and over near the home of Papa Beaver and his busy family.

My heart sank. My labs were good swimmers, but a little dog/goat in diapers and a onesie and a stream churning with frigid winter runoff filled me with fear.

With heart pounding, I threw on my boots and jacket. The yard was warming, but it was still winter in the woods. Rushing across the soggy yard, I squirmed between the chilly trees. These trees were still standing thanks to the page wire; Papa and his family had not managed to log our little forest.

The distant barking continued as I slipped and struggled down the snowy, melting, muddy slope. More than once I ended on the ground and had to grab a nearby bush to pull myself up onto my feet.

The sound of the barking grew louder and after an exhausting hike I ended up on the banks of the roaring creek.

There in the middle, on the little mud island facing the beaver lodge, barely above the churning waters stood two excited, soaked Labs in full play posture, heads and front legs bent downward and bottoms up with furiously wagging tails.

At their sides stood a small dog/goat, whose tail I was sure was also wagging. She too had her head down in play posture but was having a difficult time keeping her bottom up because her Huggie was loaded with icy stream water and dragging in the mud inside the gaping legs of her cute, soaked, pink onesie

How on earth had that little goat crossed that torrent and ended up on that tiny mud strip in front of Papa Beaver's lodge? I couldn't believe my eyes, but now I had the problem of how *I* was going to cross that raging torrent to pick up the soggy little goat and carry her to safety.

The dogs noticed me and gave me that "She's just fine, Mom, we took good care of her look!" and they went right back to happily barking and enjoying their afternoon.

Old Candy and Punkin at the mud island in Autumn.

I sent up a "Help me, Lord" prayer and with boots filling with icy water, cautiously worked my way over to the muddy strand. Picking up the shivering little goat, I felt a movement in my arms as the heavy, soaked diaper dragged the entire onesie off of Flea and it fell with a thud onto the mud. That rhymes!

I don't believe in littering, but that icy diaper was not coming back up the hill with me. I picked up the onesie, shoved the soaked kid into my jacket, and zipped up the zipper. She felt freezing cold against my shirt. I knew that I had to quickly get her back up to the house and warm her up.

The trip up the bank was grueling and I fell even more times than I had on the way down. Eventually I reached the treeline, the sunny yard, and not soon enough, the warm farm kitchen. Flea was towel-dried, wrapped in a cuddly blanket, and fed a warm bottle. She quickly drifted off to sleep dreaming of chasing cars, squirrels, and beavers and running with her dog moms to fetch the day's junk mail.

A couple of warm months passed.

"Flea is growing strong and healthy now and it might be good for her to be moved out into the barnyard with the other goats. What do you think?" I asked my husband.

"I think that that would be a good idea, the weather is warmer and it would be good for her," he replied.

That day, we moved her into the pasture and gave her a separate little goat shed for night time. The barn doors stayed open at night now and if Flea wasn't in her own little shed, I was sure that I would find her bleating desperately at the kitchen door in the middle of the night and trying to get in. I planned to still go out and give her a bedtime bottle, and we would see how this worked. For the daytime, I gifted her with a little pink sun hat, which she wore proudly. She seemed to be happy playing with her new friends. The dogs visited their little goat-pup often.

One evening, as I was feeding Flea that bedtime bottle and she was drinking happily in the doorway of her little hut, the coyote family set up a raucous howling out in the neighbouring field.

Before I could think about what was going on, two Labs bolted past me in full bark. As I turned, I saw that my bottle nipple no longer had a little goat drinking from it. I turned and stared with horror as the dogs scooted under the bottom board of the fence and a little white goat ran just behind them. I leaped from where I was and with a huge football tackle managed to grab two little back hooves as they disappeared under the fence. Flea struggled and I, face down in the barnyard muck, held on for dear life. Finally, I managed to pull the rest of the little goat back into the barnyard and cradle her in my arms. She was still wriggling and squirming to be put down. I struggled to take her bleating in frustration back to her little goat hut.

Flea was miffed and not interested in drinking the rest of her bottle, so I said "Good night," and shut the little door.

Far out in the field, the barking continued, until the howling coyotes had ceased their evening serenade.

What would that coyote family have thought if they had seen the dogs actually bringing dinner to them? Some days,

I just couldn't believe the things that went on on this little farm of ours.

Flea became a barnyard favorite and it didn't take her long to learn how to use the stiles to escape the barnyard. She'd lie adorably in the sun in front of the little log store wearing her cute sunhat. Tourists loved her, and her picture graced their photos and the front of local newspapers.

If someone set out a blanket on the lawn to have a picnic, the blanket-loving little goat would quickly join them, lie down, and with a well practiced twist, grab the corner of the blanket and pull it over her.

Did we have fleas? Yes, one tiny one, and she was adorable and loved.

How could something that started out so tiny end up having such a tremendous influence on the lives of so many people? Little children start out tiny too. Jesus loves little children and wants them to be close to him.

When his disciples tried to get the children out of the way of the adults Jesus called them unto him, and said:

Suffer little children to come unto me, and forbid them not: for of such is the kingdom of God. Lu 18:16

Flea lounging in her sun hat.

Farm Tour Saturday

Kaloka, looking in our bedroom window in the morning, "Wake up, guys, it's farm tour Saturday!"

Every day could be exciting on the farm. Any day could bring people to the store or to come to see the goats or llamas, but Saturdays could be especially busy and interesting.

Saturday always began just like the other farm days, with feeding, and watering, and milking the goats and cows. There was tidying up, shoveling out stalls, putting out fresh hay, making sure that the barnyard was nice and neat and the farmhouse yard had nicely mown grass and neat flowerbeds. Lastly, I would open the door to the little log llama store that sold so many wonderful llama and alpaca things brought from far away Peru and Ecuador.

Our little goat named Flea, loved her bright-pink sun hat but our other goats were also fond of hats and sunglasses. Many of the goats had colorful baseball caps. They often fought each other for them and would pull the hats or glasses off their friend's heads and run off. The cows preferred wide-brimmed straw hats with big bows. We had a professional photographer ask to spend a day with us photographing the animals and he took some prize-winning photos.

Yes, it sounds strange, but why wouldn't an animal hanging around in a sunny pasture on a hot day not want a nice hat with a brim and enjoy wearing sunglasses to keep the glare off?

When the clock told us that it was ten a.m., and everything was ready, we opened the big farm gates.

Soon cars and pickups began rolling down the long driveway. Grandmas and grandpas, moms and dads and lots of children happily climbed out and ran to wait outside the farm pasture gate to be let into the pasture.

"Where can we get the little bags for the llama treats?" asked one excited little boy.

"They keep them in the store," answered an elderly man who had visited many times before. "They're on the counter. Just get what you need and then you can put your quarters in the gumball machines and fill the bags with llama pellets."

The boy, along with others who had heard the directions, got the little bags off the store counter. Then they put their quarters into the machines, twisted the handles, and yummy llama treats filled their bags.

The pasture dwellers knew all about Farm Tour Saturday. When they saw the cars coming, they knew it meant that people were coming to visit. When people came, they always fed them extra treats. The llamas lined up along the fence by the gate and excitedly waited to greet the first visitors. Each llama tried to persuade the visitors to feed them from their little baggies. I could almost hear them thinking, *That one is mine, you can get treats from that one over there. Move over, I saw the little boy first. He's going to feed me!* And so it went.

The llamas often pushed and shoved each other, but when we had guests, they tried to use their best manners and wait politely.

The llama adults were taller than most full-sized men. Some, like Moses, were way taller than any man that ever came to visit. Although these large animals could certainly hurt someone, our llamas were very gentle. The farm had been the home of many of them since they were born. I could always be sure that all of our guests, even the smallest children, were perfectly safe. My little grandson Samuel had been running safely around the pasture with the llamas since he could toddle. The llamas guarded him just like he was their own.

It wasn't long before I heard a little commotion not far from the gate and saw an older man and a couple of children chasing Leah, one of my big white Saanen goats. In the background I could hear laughing and clapping.

Leah definitely had the advantage. She was lower to the ground and could turn suddenly, hide behind round bales, and then race to the other end of the pasture as quick as could be.

Nobody chases our animals! I thought as I rushed towards them to see what was going on.

A laughing grandma and some other tourists had gathered to watch the fun.

"What's going on?" I asked pleasantly, even though I was concerned for Leah.

Grandma explained through her laughter, "Grandpa always carries his money in his shirt pocket in a little clip. When he bent down to give Leah and her kids some pellets, she sniffed his pocket, grabbed the wad of twenties, and high-tailed it out into the pasture. He looked down to an empty pocket and saw Leah jumping and cavorting as she ran off with his money. He started chasing her, but I'm sure that she can outrun him! Those are our grandkids out there trying to help Grandpa get his money back."

Grandpa did want his money back, but everyone was having great fun. I chased Leah, finally caught the fun-loving goat, returned the money she had stolen, and sent her and her kids out to graze. The family and all the onlookers were now talking and laughing like old friends, and walked off together feeding friendly llamas and goats.

I was often asked questions about the animals. One common one was, "Do llamas spit?"

My reply was usually, "Do dogs bite? It is kind of the same thing. Yes, they can spit. They can't swear, or elbow, or punch, so when they get really frustrated, they will spit." But I reassured them that it didn't happen very often.

A couple with two teenagers had come to visit and they headed for one of the back pastures. This pasture was close to the farmhouse and had a nice covering of shade trees. It was here that the mommas with the younger crias rested in the afternoon. The teenaged girl was smiling as she walked with her parents amongst the adorable crias and their dams, but the young man had an attitude and didn't seem like he wanted to be there at all. He went up to Kaloka, one of my tall llama mommas, and raised his chin up to look her straight in the eyes. He shoved his face right up to hers and then began pretending that he was chewing. That was a very rude thing to do in the llama book of manners. If a llama is really upset and planning to spit, it will look like it's chewing and will bring up some nasty stuff ready to spit with.

Now I could see that this young man was seriously angering this tall, gentle momma. He was chewing right in her face and so she began doing the same. I could tell by the position of her ears that she was downright fed up.

I warned him, "Don't do that to her, she's going to spit on you. You're getting her angry!"

The young man ignored me with a snorty laugh. Suddenly, Kaloka raised her head, pinned her ears back, flung her head forward, and fired not once but four times. He was covered in smelly green slime. He glared at me, angrily wiping yucky green grass chunks and slippery vomit out of his eyes and off his cheeks.

"I warned you," I said defending my usually quiet girl.

He scowled angrily at his parents and sister. They were standing there grinning. Grumbling and saying some not very polite words, he stomped back to the car, and the rest of the family continued enjoying their afternoon.

As people visited the various pastures I dashed back into the store where folks were mulling around and shopping for special things.

The kids loved the Peruvian instruments, the teddy bears, and other colorful items. The moms shopped for beautiful, very soft, llama and Alpaca clothing. As I was waiting on my customers, I overheard a conversation happening right outside the store window.

There was a little pen there and the llamas liked to hang around so that they could be closer to the store customers and beg for more treats. I couldn't help but peek out the window so that I could listen.

Our towering guardian, Moses, had entered the pen and was looking down at three elderly women. He was almost twice as tall as they were.

The ladies all wore flowered sun hats over their grey hair. They had on flowered shirts and khaki shorts down to their knees with knee socks folded over at the tops and hiking boots. They looked like they were ready for any adventure that could come their way.

I looked over at Moses, who as you know was very intelligent and always very thoughtful. I could tell by his eyes that he too was curious about these three unique ladies.

The adventurer closest to the store stood staring intently, looking over my big boy from top to bottom. Then, with awe-filled eyes, she confidently and loudly stated,

"They lay really big eggs you know!"

I couldn't help but grin, and noticed that poor Moses stared at these ladies with a confused expression on his muzzle.

The lady next to the one who had spoken nodded her head in approval and added, "We live near a farm, and they have lots of these, and they lay really big eggs!" She held her hands in a position to show the other ladies what she meant by "big." Her egg size would have made a dinosaur proud.

Finally, the third lady, with a look of disgust, decided that she would have to set these two straight. With her head wagging from side to side, and her finger pointing and making wide sideways swoops across her flowered shirt, she boldly argued, "No they don't! 'They don't lay eggs!" They just have their babies like other animals!"

I thought I saw Moses breathe a sigh of relief. Not too long ago a young couple had asked if he was a good milker.

The first two ladies continued to argue about the eggs while the third loudly argued back and then, with an angry screech yelled, "You two are getting them mixed up with those bird things. They also have long necks and they DO lay eggs!"

Before I had to go out and settle the argument, they huffed at each other, and the two egg-laying fans went off in one direction while the other headed off in another. Later in the day as they walked toward the gate, I heard them talking to each other with words like "deary," "sweety" and "love," so I knew that all was well once again.

In the middle of the afternoon I brought out the llama toys. They were really baby toys for children under three years old. But the llamas, who were very intelligent creatures, loved to play with them. We used the clicker training method. Melody ran for the toy bag and the llamas looked over to where we were with delight.

The first toy that I brought out was the first one that they were trained with. It was a colorful little clown that was all squished and grew to his full size with a big boing sound when the button on the top of his hat was pushed. When the llamas heard the sound of that little clown, they all came running to join in on the fun. The pasture wanderers soon followed the galloping herd to where I was setting up, to watch, laugh, and clap as the llamas just enjoyed themselves.

Four or five wooly llamas came up close to me, almost knocking me over as they reached out with their long necks to get a turn at poking the button with their noses and making the clown boing and grow. Of course, our herd of more than thirty playful llamas could not all get a turn on everything, so after giving many turns, I set the clown in the bag and picked up a small keyboard.

Jaycee and Penny were not going to miss out and so they shoved their muzzles in my bag and began fighting over the clown's button where it lay amongst the other toys. Jaycee pulled backwards to take the bag for herself and caught her head in the handles. As she jumped up in surprise, toys scattered over the pasture.

Melody chased down the naughty llama. "Come here, you," she scolded. "You can't have all the toys for yourself, you have to share!"

Meanwhile, Penny had found the little clown lying on the grass and was banging her nose against it to make it boing.

Melody picked up the favorite toy and put it into the toy bag. Both Penny and Jaycee followed right at her shoulders begging her to let them play some more.

"Take out the flute," I called to her, knowing that she could distract them. The llamas had easily learned to blow in the little flute. Melody knew how to cover the buttons to let them make the music, but they were all virtuosos and wanted to play endlessly. Orangy-red Juanita saw the flute appear and pushed in to persuade Melody to let her play.

While Melody tried to get the llamas to share the flute, I offered the little keyboard to some others. It was another favourite; the llamas could play it by using their split upper lip like fingers. The music was pretty bad, but they loved it. I usually had to stop each one because they would just keep playing and there were a lot of llamas waiting to take a turn.

We had quite a few toys, most with buttons where pushing the correct button would make music play or lights flash. One of the more difficult toys that I introduced to them at about four months had two sets of buttons. It had cartooned faces of a mommy, daddy, grandma, grandpa, and baby, and a dog, cat, and bird. If the top button was pushed, a lower one said the words, daddy, baby, etc. Some of the llamas could push the button for the correct picture after I had said it to them and then press the button for the correct word to go along with it. Their noses banged on the toy as they struggled between each other to be the llama who pushed the right button and got the treat. The toy would repeat the word if it was correct and play a little song. Then the llama would get lots of praise and a treat. It was difficult to have one llama using the learning toy without another winding its long neck over my shoulder and pushing the correct button first.

Pokey, one of our young show llamas, also had a favorite toy. It had four big colored buttons and when each was pushed lights would flash and a different song would play. Llamas see colors and so I could name the color and she would push it and then the tune would play.

I took Pokey to a nearby school one day, and she was performing a lot of tricks for the kids and staff. There was even a news reporter there. The last trick of our little performance was the toy with the big buttons. I thought that I would have children call out a color and then have my prize llama push it and play the tune for them. I asked for a child to call out one of the colors.

"Red," he said.

Pokey ignored him and pushed the blue button. The blue button played "The Muffin Man."

"Red, Pokey, Red," I repeated encouragingly. I tried a number of times, but she would only push the blue button. I couldn't believe this. She was so good at this trick! "The

Muffin Man" played over and over. I was very embarrassed, and then I noticed that the staff and children were laughing and clapping for the naughty llama.

Finally, a little five-year-old boy stood up and through his giggles explained, "But she likes "The Muffin Man.""

Everybody clapped.

The photographer took our pictures and pictures of the laughing audience, and Pokey and I headed home. I guess the children could relate to a young llama who wanted her own way.

Pokey, as stubborn as she could be, loved buttons. I really had to watch her with the tourists when they had their cameras out. It was obvious that she wanted to be a photographer.

I was taking a picture of a new cria one morning when the camera was grabbed out of my hands by Miss Pokey. She swung her long neck up out of my reach and then used that special movable top lip of hers to push the button and actually take some pictures. The camera flashed and then the willful llama ran off with my camera and I had to chase her for it. I couldn't help but wonder if the pictures would actually turn out.

This was before cellphones when cameras had rolls of film in them. When the roll was finished the girls and I took the film in to be developed.

"Don't throw away any pictures that are blurry." Melody requested at the camera shop. "A llama took a couple of pictures but didn't hold the camera still. It's probably blurry."

The attendant looked at us kind of funny, but nodded his head.

"Yes," I added. "It may be the only picture ever taken by a llama!"

The pictures were developed and sure enough, there was a blurry picture taken by an inspired llama and I proudly have it to this day.

On Farm Tour Saturday, as the little demonstration was ending and toys were going back into my bag, Pokey took up position for the last performance of the day. On a large piece of plywood, I had painted a Peruvian man and woman in their full native costumes, holding a pretty llama between them. The picture was life-sized and holes had been cut where the faces would have been. The farm guests loved to have their pictures taken while standing behind it with their faces showing through the holes.

Pokey had a special part in their pictures. She had been trained to push her face into one of the holes and hold it there very still while someone stood beside her with their face in the other hole. This brought a lot of laughter from everyone watching because at least one of the Peruvian people in the picture would be quite funny looking. There were a lot of line ups to get their pictures taken with Pokey's big nose sticking through one of the faces.

While the photographs were being taken, I noticed that some of the crowd was laughing and heading quickly over towards the gate. I soon found out why. Just outside the farm gate was a pop machine. It was popular on hot days. Two young men were standing by the gate with cans of cold root beer. *Okay,* I thought, *that's not exciting.* But then I saw what was really going on. Two of my juvenile boys were right in there and Avi's soft nose was sniffing right at the bottom of the can as one of the fellows drank.

The young man looked at the friendly little llama and asked, "Want a drink?" and with that he tipped the can gently into the little fellow's eager mouth. I'm sure that he thought that the llama would refuse.

Avi startled at the fizz and then began to suck root beer from the can. Everyone began laughing. The other young man tried the same with Willy and by the time I reached the happy crowd, two four-month-old llamas were holding the ends of cans of root beer in their mouths and guzzling like pros.

I yelled, "Hey," and ran up, but the cans had dropped and much to the delight of the crowd, Avi actually let out a big burp.

"You can't feed root beer to the llamas! It's not healthy for them," I instructed.

Everybody was still tittering.

Later, I put up a sign. "No Pop for the Llamas!" The little llamas couldn't read of course, and begged endlessly whenever anyone entered the pasture with a cold drink.

It was almost time to bid our guests goodbye and shut the farm gate, but there was more excitement in the pasture. The grandfather and his grandkids were now chasing Leah's twin kids from this spring; Homer and Herman. The kids were even faster than their mother. The laughing crowd told me that before leaving, the grandpa had bent to pet Leah's twins and they grabbed the wad of twenties out of his shirt pocket and ran.

We chased the little thieves and returned the money to the grandfather.

"You've trained them to do this!" he said with a twinkle in his eye. "It would be easier if you just raised your farm fee."

The grandfather and his family and the rest of the visitors left laughing and I closed the gate. Time for farm chores and then dinner.

There was one more trick that I could use the llamas' help with. That was cleaning up the pasture of little bits of paper and garbage. I had trained a few of them to pick up paper and then drop it over a garbage can. Very convenient.

They happily picked up and dropped, but I couldn't get them to drop it deep enough in the can and the breeze would usually blow it away with me chasing it. I actually think they could have done better, but they really liked seeing me chasing blowing paper over the grass while they stood and chewed their cud.

After dinner, I looked out. The sun was beginning to set and in the end, it had been a perfect day. The pastures were peaceful, with the llamas all lying down in "cush" position with their front legs bent underneath them and ready to head to dreamland. All that is, except one. Taya was still busy. She must have wanted a bedtime snack because she was standing in front of one of the treat machines. Her mouth was wide open with her lower jaw held under the chute where the treats would come out. Those two special lips were latched onto the turning knob. She was working those lips to turn that knob as hard as she could, but of course no llama treats would pour down the chute into her waiting mouth. I smiled, shook my head, and wondered, *Should I take her a quarter?*

A merry heart doeth good like a medicine: Proverbs 17:22

Homer says, "There's always next time!"
Photo Credit: Brechin Mclaine.

Buzzard and the Chimney Sweep

Buzzard, my baby.

Buzzard was a very big turkey. We weighed him once and he was more than fifty pounds. He had come to live at the farm just a few days after he had hatched from an egg. When he was tiny, I used to pick him up and stroke his little feathers as they grew. Then I'd set him gently back with the other little turkeys under the warm lights in the sawdust-filled box. When he had grown big enough that I had to hold him with two hands, I set him upon a little perch in the chicken coop every night and said, "Goodnight, baby."

We had received six little turkeys, but Buzzard was my special boy. He happily followed me around the farm and although farm visitors were terrified of him when he had grown to full size, he was really very gentle and friendly.

He loved music and along with his turkey flock, the dogs, and a few chickens used to parade across the lawn following Melody, who like the pied piper, played lovely tunes on her flute as she walked.

One day, when my three-year-old granddaughter Abby visited us, she found herself face to face with a turkey who was as tall as she was.

I looked out the patio window opened the sliding door and called out, "It's okay, sweetie. He won't hurt you!"

The standoff continued with each staring straight into the other's eyes.

"He loves music, honey," I called to the tiny, adorable blond who was bravely holding her ground without flinching. "Sing to him and you will make him happy."

Well the next thing I knew, that sweet, blue-eyed darling was tearing across the lawn, while turning to watch Buzzard who was trying to keep up. At the top of her little lungs Abby was singing, "JESUS LOVES ME THIS I KNOW!"

She reached the closest fence, scrambled up to the top rail and continued to serenade the happy turkey, who was pacing back and forth near her dangling feet and enjoying the music. What an amazing, special child, what a delightful turkey!

One day, a van with ladders hooked onto the sides, drove down the long driveway. A rather dirty little man climbed out of the cab and came up to the door. "I'm here to clean your fireplace chimney just like you asked!" he stated.

He was a chimney sweep, and got busy right away leaning one of his ladders against the side of the house so that he could climb up onto the roof. Once the ladder was in place, he pulled his special brushes out of the back of his van along with a box of tools that he would need on the roof. Up he climbed.

Buzzard had brought the whole turkey flock over to watch. He looked up at the little man on the roof with his friendly turkey smile.

The chimney sweep looked down at the little turkey flock with a scowl. He didn't like animals and turkeys were only good to be put on a dinner plate. "Heh! Get out of here!" he ordered nastily as he looked downward.

Squeezing his brooms down the hole in the chimney, he forced them up and down a few times and made billowing clouds of sooty dust fly into the air.

It wasn't long before he decided that he was finished and looked over the edge to see where he could throw his brooms down. He scowled. The whole little flock of turkeys was standing at the bottom of the ladder. *Oh well* he seemed to think with a nasty smile on his face, *they'll move when these brooms come flying down.* He reached for the first broom, which had a strange circle of bristles all around the bottom. He dropped it and it landed bristles down.

The flock fluttered and scattered, but not before the broom handle had bopped trusting Buzzard right on the top of his head.

The chimney sweep apparently didn't care, and he reached for the second broom, hurling it down onto the ground.

From the large sliding glass doors, I watched in disbelief but was too late to stop what had just taken place. I could see that Buzzard cared! He was angry. He was very angry and his head and neck began changing color: blue, red, blue and bright red as he stared upward with beady turkey eyes. In his anger, he began to gobble words that you or I would likely not want to hear. His large wings began to rise and rattle to attention.

I ran to the back door in time to glimpse the chimney sweep barreling down the ladder and kicking his dirty boot at poor Buzzard. Buzzard let out an angry gobble squawk, spread his long wings out even farther, and leaped into the air. He turned his big tummy towards the sweep, showing his huge talons and long, spikey leg claws

Now the chimney sweep knew that he was in trouble. He almost threw his tool box away and began running across the yard as fast as he could with a very angry turkey right on his heels. The man managed to loop around, and in a panic, jumped into his van. Buzzard began pacing and patrolling outside the door.

I knew that I had to step in and rescue the man, so I held Buzzard, whose turkey heart was still pounding, and comforted him with soft words. I motioned for the terrified man to get out and grab his tool box and brooms. He grabbed them in a flash, all the while keeping his eye on poor Buzzard. Then he jumped into his van and flew down the driveway.

That night as I hoisted my fifty-pound "baby" onto his perch, I commented, "It's sure too bad that man didn't know anything about kindness! Goodnight, baby."

Be ye kind one to another. Ephesians 4:32

Buzzard looked up with his friendly turkey smile

THE REAL TAILS OF EASY YOKE FARM

Billowing clouds of sooty dust flew into the air.

His broom bopped Buzzard right on his head.

The chimney sweep knew that he was in trouble.

The Stallion and the Buck

The days weren't always peaceful on the farm. Once in a while some of the animals took a dislike to one of their barnyard companions and a small pasture war began.

As you know, a dozen or so lovely nanny goats and their kids enjoyed one of our pastures, along with a buck named Isaac. Isaac had grown into a handsome white buck, with a shiny, long white coat and a beautiful long beard. The fact that he was the head goat and the biggest didn't mean that the nanny goats didn't push him around when they felt like it

The pasture beside them was occupied by Melody's handsome palomino, Prince, and a fiery red stallion named Spitfire.

The horses, bored by their inactivity, spent much time lazily hanging over the fence line watching the antics of the ever-busy goat herd.

There was always something going on in the goat pasture; from the jumping and running of the tireless goat kids, to the daily sparring and playing of the nannies.

It struck me that the horses, because of their many hours of observation couldn't help but notice things that the goat family could improve upon. I heard the frustrated, snorting neighs even from the farmhouse. Certainly, they wished that the nannies should not allow their kids to jump around on the hay bales and then soil them. They should not reach over and chew the bark on the farmer's flowering bushes, and my goodness, but that buck should take a bath in the pond once in a while!

So, while the horses filled their days observing, and (I imagined) discussing ways that they would improve upon the lives and behaviors of their goat neighbours, they casually reached over the fence line that divided the pastures and ate the grass that grew there.

The buck goat, Isaac, considered this intrusion into his pasture by this murmuring, criticizing pair more than he could tolerate in a Christian spirit. On one fine morning as I entered the goat pasture to do chores, I noticed Isaac carefully eyeing the munchers. Then, approaching the fence, he warned them by rearing up, and making a butting motion with his head.

Prince promptly removed his head and neck from the goat pasture and took a step backwards to observe what would happen next.

Spitfire snorted back at Isaac, and with a disdainful glare went right back to eating on the wrong side of the fence.

Isaac had no difficulty in deciding what to do next. He felt that he was the head of the herd, even if the goat ladies didn't always treat him like the head. He knew that he was much bigger than this horse's neck and head! He took aim, lowered his head, charged forward, suddenly reared up with a twist and then smashed down on Spitfire's nose driving it back into the boards. He then stood his ground to see if this rude intruder would leave.

Spitfire shook his head and snorted; partly because of the smell, then eyed the angry buck goat thoughtfully. With calm execution, he reached toward Isaac, grabbed him by the scruff of the neck, picked him up off the grass, and then held him there, dangling.

Isaac, who was hanging with all of his hooves off the ground, seethed. Spitfire dropped him and stood glaring, waiting to see if the determined buck would retreat.

Isaac backed off, charged towards the fence, reared up, and smashed Spitfire's nose against the boards. Spitfire reached over, grabbed the buck by the back of his thick neck, and swung him upwards until his feet hung once more.

Isaac dangled defiantly.

Spitfire dropped him.

I couldn't believe my eyes. Here were these two strong-willed animals actually hurting each other and still determined to get their own ways.

Isaac charged—*wham!*

Spitfire picked him up, hung him momentarily, then dropped him.

Smash! The bitter buck rammed that nose. Up went the goat, down he fell with a thud.

Bam went his hard head against that nose.

Up into the air went Isaac, and *bang* he dropped onto the ground.

I stood amazed by this endless battle. Shaking my head, an idea came to me. I would have to do something to distract these two before they hurt each other. I approached the fence where the fight was still raging and opened the gate between the two pastures. For a brief time, all was still. The pastures were motionless. Suddenly, the bell-clad nannies and their kids made a quick run through the gate and clambered toward the horse's round bale. Prince also made a hasty pass into the now-empty goat pasture and turned back to watch this new development from a distance.

Isaac and Spitfire eyed each other warily. Isaac realized that the fence that kept the other part of Spitfire in check was no longer between them. Spitfire, meanwhile, was considering how his belly might feel if that goat had a mind to bash him again. Looking around, both offenders suddenly realized that because of their fighting, they had lost the thing that they thought they were fighting for—their own pasture.

Where would they go? I could tell that they were quite confused at this new situation. They couldn't really go anywhere; they both belonged to our family.

They walked around each other delicately. Isaac was beginning to feel some pain where the horse's strong teeth had repeatedly grabbed him.

Spitfire acknowledged a throbbing pain in his long nose. Both began planning ways to survive in the joint pasture and nurse their wounds. Meanwhile they'd keep a careful eye out for the one that they not only mistrusted, but blamed for the loss of their pasture.

On the other hand, I had only just begun my plan to bring peace to the pasture. I began setting the food out in just one spot, and keeping just one water tank full. Before long, the horses and goats could be seen eating together peacefully. The goat kids discovered that sunbathing horses made great hills and the horses began to find the fluffy little creatures eased a lot of their boredom. They actually found that they were so cute and winsome that discovering that you were nose to nose with one when you were eating off the very top of a round bale really wasn't so bad after all.

One night when the coyotes entered the pasture, bent on no good, Isaac realized that the big horses sent the coyotes running for the fence line. Was it his imagination, or were things actually better now that everyone was living together as a family instead of criticizing and fighting with each other?

Slowly the hurt and mistrust were forgotten and the farm became a place of unity and joy.

If it is possible, try as hard as you can
to live in peace with everyone.
Romans 12:18 (paraphrase)

Blossom's Temper

Blossom, Buttercup's baby, had grown quickly into a very large cow with a nice brown coat with big white patches. She had big brown eyes, and two little horns that grew between her soft floppy ears. She had a long tail with three long ringlet curls of hair that almost reached the ground. Blossom was a gentle cow, but both flies and humans had to beware when that long tail swished. It stung!

Blossom all grown up.

When Blossom was about two years old, she became old enough to begin milking. Thomas put her halter on her and led her to a stall in the barn where we had covered the floor with clean straw. Her halter and lead were hooked to the manger, which was her dinner dish. I had already filled it with lots of nice grain and molasses poured onto some fresh alfalfa hay.

Blossom happily munched as Thomas and I placed the shiny milk pail underneath her udder and sat down on the upturned white buckets that we used as milking stools. She was a very wide cow and so one of us needed to milk from each side of her.

"She's standing nicely," I commented to Thomas as her first warm milk began to squirt noisily into the metal bucket.

"Yes, she is," he replied. "This might be easier than I thought it would be."

"Good girl, Blossom."

Blossom stood and milked like the perfect cow, until the yummy grain was all gone. Then, she began to pull on her lead and stomp, buck, and swish that long whip of a tail to hit anyone near her.

"Whoa, settle down girl," Thomas cried, and we both stood up and jumped back to avoid being swatted or kicked.

She wouldn't settle down, and she finally brought a big hoof forward and then back, kicking the bucket and sending the fresh milk all over the barn floor. She wanted to go running out in the pasture and she wasn't going to wait any longer! That was the end of milking that morning.

That evening, at milking time, Blossom behaved the same way and kicked the milk bucket once again; shoving a filthy hoof right inside of it before sending it flying.

The next morning, Blossom carried on just as badly. She was a very impatient cow. This wasn't working.

Finally, we called an old farmer friend. "We've got this milk cow," I began, "who begins to buck and kick and dump all the milk as soon as she's finished eating her grain. She's a big cow and we just don't know what to do to settle her down and train her. Can you help us out?"

"Don't worry," our friend comforted us. "I know exactly what to do. I'll come down at seven after milking."

Thomas and I breathed a sigh of relief and looked forward to getting some help.

Around seven, the farmer showed up carrying a long piece of rope and an old, battered milk bucket. "Bring Blossom back into the stall and give her some fresh hay," he instructed.

Blossom came willingly, looking forward to some more grain. As she ate, the farmer tied the top of the rope to a hook in the barn ceiling so that the rope hung close to Blossom's legs but didn't touch them. Then he tied the old milk bucket onto the end of the rope, close to Blossom's back legs, but still not touching them. He stood back looking very pleased.

It didn't take long before Blossom finished eating her hay. As usual, she began pulling and trying to yank herself loose. She moved backwards and her leg touched the bucket.

Blossom had had some experience in dealing with troublesome milk buckets! She gave it a hard kick. The bucket swung backwards, but then something happened that surprised our impatient cow. The bucket swung back on its rope and hit her in the hind end.

Blossom mooed and jumped angrily, kicking the old bucket even harder. It swung back farther and flew back to hit her—hard.

Thomas and I looked at each other and suddenly we understood what the old farmer was trying to do. Blossom was going to discipline herself. We decided to leave the barn and we walked our farmer friend out to his pickup.

"Let me know how this turns out," he said with a twinkle in his eyes and he left for home.

For hours we heard the smashing of the bucket and the loud mooing of an impatient and angry cow.

In the morning, as we woke, the farm was quiet.

"I don't hear anything," Thomas commented, sitting up in bed.

"Neither do I," I replied. "Do you think she's all right?"

"Probably," he answered and we got up and got ready to head to the barn.

There, in a perfectly peaceful barn, we discovered a calm Blossom standing and patiently waiting. A very dented and still bucket hung from the rafters.

"Good morning, Blossom," Thomas said with a grin. "Did you have a good sleep last night?"

We filled the manger with sweet grain and hay and cautiously placed the shiny milk pail under her udder. At the same time, we kept a watchful eye out for that whip of a tail that stung so much when it hit.

"She's doing so much better," I said to Thomas.

"So far," he answered, glancing up at the manger that was quickly emptying.

We milked and milked.

Blossom finished eating and stood quietly until we were finished.

"Good girl, Blossom," we both said and let her loose to graze in the pasture.

Blossom never kicked the bucket again. She had learned to stand patiently. The bucket had won.

But let patience have [her] perfect work, that ye may be perfect and entire, wanting nothing. James 1:4

Farm fun!

Peanut Butter Toast

One morning after breakfast, I noticed a nice piece of peanut butter toast still sitting on a breakfast plate.

I don't want to throw it in the garbage, I thought. *Maybe if I set it out on the sundeck railing, a shiny black raven or a noisy bluejay will swoop down and have it for breakfast. Besides, it's cold outside and peanut butter toast could make a little bird's tummy warm again.*

I carefully put the piece of peanut butter toast on the porch railing and looked around slowly. *No birds yet,* I thought.

I went back into the warm kitchen to tidy up. Around lunchtime, I looked out on the porch to see if the peanut butter toast had disappeared. It was still there.

Oh well, I thought, *Maybe they don't know what peanut butter toast is. Maybe they don't know how yummy it is.*

"Maybe they don't like peanut butter toast!" said Thomas.

All afternoon, the peanut butter toast sat on the porch rail. Not one bird seemed to want it.

The next morning, when I peeked out the door, a big change had taken place. There were tiny little bites all around the edge of the peanut butter toast. They were so neat, it looked just like someone had decorated it. I thought maybe it was the bushy-tailed squirrel or even the neighbour's cat. Every time I looked out the window there were more neat little bites out of the peanut butter toast. There wasn't one bite here and another one there—they were all in the neatest little rows. Who was eating the peanut butter toast?

All through the day, I kept peeking out the kitchen window, but no one was there. *How can this be? Who could come and go so quickly that I can't catch them?*

By the time the sky grew dark and the chilly winter wind began to howl, the toast had been scraped perfectly clean.

The next morning, I was very, very curious. Today, I would be sure to find out who was enjoying the peanut butter toast!

"Has anyone been eating your peanut butter toast?" Thomas asked.

"Oh yes, they're eating it all up, well at least they are eating the peanut butter all up!"

I got out a knife and spread a big blob of yummy peanut butter all over the empty piece of toast on the ledge. *Maybe it's the little brown sparrows, or a pretty yellow grosbeak, or a lovely purple finch?* Whoever it was, they were very fast and very neat.

All day long, the peanut butter vanished in neat little bites until it was scraped clean and I still didn't know who was eating the peanut butter toast.

THE REAL TAILS OF EASY YOKE FARM

The mystery was getting bigger each day. I just had to know! I put out a new piece of warm toast and covered it with thick, gooey peanut butter that smelled so good.

Then, I pulled up a chair close to the window, hid it just behind the lacy curtains, and sat down. Before long, someone did come to the porch to taste the peanut butter. It was the bushy-tailed squirrel.

He tiptoed close to the toast, looked around carefully, and sniffed with his tiny squirrel nose. I could barely wait to see what would happen next. He put out his little squirrel tongue, took one long lick, and made a little tongue mark. Suddenly, he scampered away. He didn't leave the nice neat bites that I had been watching for. Well, now I knew that it wasn't the bushy-tailed brown squirrel that liked peanut butter toast.

A pretty, bright-blue blue jay seemed to jump out of nowhere. *Ah hah!* I thought. *Maybe he's the one who loves peanut butter toast.*

The blue jay stepped carefully over to the toast. He cocked his perky little head and turned so his bright black eyes could take a good look. Slowly he reached his beak towards the toast and grabbed it. He couldn't bite through it and when he tried to pick it up it fell off the railing and onto the porch. This was just too much work for the blue jay and he quickly flew away.

I got up, went outside, and carefully put the toast back on the railing. The blue jay was not the one who was eating the peanut butter toast.

Once more I sat down behind the lace curtains to watch. Suddenly, a little bird with a black cap on its head came and perched near the toast. He took a bite, and then another, and another, all in tiny neat rows. When he left, his friends all flew down, and finished one neat row after another. What careful little birds. No one took a bite out of line. Soon the toast was scraped clean and the little flock flew home to their nests with tummies full of delicious peanut butter. The mystery was solved. The chickadees were eating the peanut butter toast.

Thomas," I called excitedly. "We have a flock of peanut butter chickadees!"

Every morning, while the snow was on the ground, I toasted a little piece of toast; just for the hungry little birds. I covered it with yummy peanut butter and set it carefully on the ledge. Every morning, all winter long, the tiny, black-capped chickadees waited patiently in the lilac bush. When they saw me open the kitchen door, they began to sing a joyful, "Chickadee dee dee. Chickadee dee dee."

I smiled a big welcoming smile and said, "Good morning, peanut butter chickadees, Enjoy your peanut butter toast!" I love the little birds and wanted to make sure that they were well taken care of.

God loves the little birds but loves us so much more and tells us that we don't have to be afraid because he will take care of us.

THE REAL TAILS OF EASY YOKE FARM

Look at the birds of the air: they neither sow nor reap nor gather into barns, and yet your heavenly Father feeds them. Are you not of more value than they? Matthew 6:25

The peanut butter vanished in neat little bites.

Jujube

Jujube was a tiny, newborn goat. He was a rare breed and he was very valuable. Jujube was not our little goat. He was born on another farm where his mother had died.

His owners brought him to us wrapped in a little towel and pleaded with us to help them. As they handed the little fellow to me, they sadly told us, "We don't know what to do, he won't drink from a bottle, and he's so weak that he can't even stand up. Maybe one of your goats would feed him. His name is Jujube." They said this softly as they turned for one more look at their little goat and then walked slowly to their truck.

As his owners left, Melody and I stood gazing at the shivering little goat

"This little goat can't be put into the barnyard," I said softly to Melody. "Can you find me a little box that we can use for a bed?" Melody found a little box and we lined it with soft doll blankets.

I felt Jujube's little body. His legs were stiff and unmovable. "It's no wonder he can't stand," I told Melody. "I'm sure that he has white muscle disease. They couldn't have known that the soil around here is low in selenium and all of the animals have to have a supplement. I'll have to phone them and tell them to get a selenium lick for their other goats or they'll all end up like Jujube. Where's the thermometer?"

Melody brought it to me and I took Jujube's temperature. It was much too high. *This is beginning to make sense,* I thought. I put my ear on his little chest, and I could hear weak, rattling little breaths.

"He also has pneumonia, I told Melody sadly. "We have our work cut out for us. This little goat is also going to need a lot of prayer."

We kept him warm in a little box and gave him selenium supplements along with some healthy herbs and vitamins that he needed to get healthy again. I also gave him injections of penicillin. Our family prayed for him at family time.

After a few days, the fever began to go down, and Jujube slowly began to accept a small amount of the warm bottles of goat milk that we offered him. It took almost two weeks before he could move his spindly legs and stand up. For weeks, he stayed in the house wearing diapers and being bottle fed like a little baby. He slept in Melody's bed with her and she gently fed him whenever he was hungry. Eventually his breathing returned to normal and he was able to stand and walk.

One day we carried him out to the barnyard and introduced him to a small mother goat named Minnie May. She had been given to us recently from another farm after her baby had died. Minnie May saw the tiny goat with the brown ears and reached over to sniff him. I set him underneath her udder and tried to get him to latch on.

"Come on, Jujube, try this," Melody and I urged. "It's good. Over here a bit, this is how all of the other little goats drink their milk." We had made sure that he was hungry.

Minnie May seemed pleased and kept looking back as if to say, *I hope he wants to have some of my milk.*

Eventually, after some wiggling and struggling, Jujube began drinking from Minnie May and both little goats seemed very happy.

We still couldn't leave Jujube in the barn yard, though, because he was still a bit weak. So we carried him back into the house.

Many times a day he was carried to the barnyard and Minnie May bleated at him as she watched us carry him over the stile. We could tell that she had adopted him as her own goat kid. After a few months when he became frisky and healthy, we left him in the barnyard with his new goat mommy.

But little Jujube's problems were not over. He was different. He didn't really belong in our barnyard. My goats had all white ears. His were a soft brown and were so long that he tripped on them when he ran. My goats told him in no uncertain terms that they didn't like his ears and they bit and pulled them.

My goats had straight white noses. He had a flat little face almost like a bunny rabbit so they pushed him away from the feed and were very rude. My goats were tall with long legs and long hair. Jujube had short powerful little legs and short fur.

My goats went *Baaaa*. Jujube cried *maaaaam*, and sounded just like a child. My goats pushed and butted and bit his tail. I told them many times that Jujube was going to grow up to be the king of someone's barnyard, but they just kept on being mean.

Jujube's new goat mother loved him, though. She was one of my smallest goats, but she stuck up for him and protected him as best she could.

Jujube grew up anyway and became strong and healthy. He was a very powerful goat and could easily have made the other goats behave, but he was very patient and calmly put up with their meanness. He never pushed back or bit, but stayed kind and gentle.

One day, he went back to his own barnyard to live. His goat family there was very glad to see him and saw that he was the biggest and strongest of them all. He was loved and respected.

Many months passed and one day two of my goat ladies were invited to pay Jujube a visit in his barnyard; just to see how he was doing.

They were shocked and possibly very embarrassed. Just as they had been told, Jujube was the king of his barnyard and the farmer was very pleased with him and treated him with great love.

All the other goats in Jujube's barnyard had long brown ears and rounded faces. They had short powerful legs, short soft fur; and they all looked beautiful. My goats felt out of place and I imagined they didn't feel very pretty at all.

When King Jujube came to eat, all of the other goats backed away from the feeder out of respect. Nobody butted or pushed him.

My goat ladies looked very uncomfortable when they stood before him. I think they wished that they had listened many months before when they were told how special Jujube was and that he really was a king.

Many years ago, a weak little baby was sent from his world into ours. He was given a human mother to care for him and he was born in someone else's barnyard. He too was very valuable. He too was a king. His mother loved him, but he too was different because he never did anything bad. He never sinned. His name was Jesus, the King—God's son.

As Jesus grew up, he was laughed at and treated very badly. Nobody believed who he was. Even though he was good and kind, he was pushed around. When he was grown up, he got arrested. They beat him and said very mean things to him. They hurt him so bad that nobody could recognize who he was. Finally, they murdered him by hanging him on a cross. Jesus was innocent, good, and kind, but he put up with all the meanness and died for our sins.

He didn't stay dead but came alive and went back to His Father, God, in his own home in Heaven. Everyone there worships and honors him.

Just like my two unbelieving goat ladies, we will all stand before our King Jesus. Will we be delighted to see our King, or will we be ashamed because we really haven't treated him like a king at all? Do we worship and honor him or do we use his name as a swear word? Do we give ourselves to him or push him out of the way and do as we please? How will we feel when we stand before King Jesus?

For it is written, As I live, saith the Lord,
every knee shall bow to me,
and every tongue shall confess to God. Romans 14: 11

Peaceful sunrise.
Photo credits to Brechin Mclaine.

About the Author

In the not-so-distant past, Rosemary and her family retired to a small farm with a desire for clean country air, homegrown food, and a more relaxed rural lifestyle. As city folks they arrived naive but armed with a love of God, each other, and animals. It was their lack of country smarts that led them to run their farm in a unique and wonderful way that produced special animals and this charming but true story.

Rosemary has always been active in volunteer and church-related activities, especially but not limited to those involving children. She has written many short stories, for children and adults, as well as devotionals and Bible studies. While at the farm she wrote monthly articles for a llama periodical, often of a comical nature about barnyard goings-on, and she also included many llama and animal cartoons for the same. Her cartoons have been commissioned, published in various locations, and are enjoyed as prints and original works hanging proudly in their owners' homes.

She has published two books of poetry and continues writing and sharing poetry with others. With a fully-grown family, Rosemary and Tom, her husband, now enjoy many grandchildren and some great-grandchildren.

CPSIA information can be obtained
at www.ICGtesting.com
Printed in the USA
BVHW022253211120
593541BV00012B/19